"I don't think there is a better book on spiritual warfare. ... through the confusion and fear that so often attend this topic with practical biblical insight, carefully given by a skilled surgeon of the soul. Every Christian should read this book so they are prepared for the inevitable battles they will face between the 'already' of their conversion and the 'not yet' of their home-going."

Paul David Tripp, President of Paul Tripp Ministries; pastor; best-selling author of *New Morning Mercies*

"During his lifetime, David Powlison gave to the church gifts too numerous to mention. His parting gift of this book is no exception. Using Ephesians 6 as a foundation, David makes a compelling case for Christian life and ministry as everyday spiritual warfare empowered by the Divine Warrior himself, our triune God. This is warfare demystified—battle against the world, the flesh, and the devil waged prayerfully and dependently on your knees with Scripture in your hand and your heart."

Michael R. Emlet, Counselor and Dean of Faculty, Christian Counseling & Educational Foundation (CCEF); author of *CrossTalk: Where Life and Scripture Meet* and *Descriptions and Prescriptions: A Biblical Perspective on Psychiatric Diagnoses and Medications*

"*Safe and Sound* protects you from the worst kind of spiritual warfare where you let Satan 'get in your head.' We have the high ground. That's one of David Powlison's many rich insights in this thoughtful book on fighting the powers of darkness. Taking spiritual warfare seriously does not mean letting Satan shape the narratives around his power. He's a defeated enemy, with a fatal wound from the death and resurrection of Jesus Christ!"

Paul E. Miller, Director of seeJesus; author of *A Praying Life* and *J-Curve: Dying and Rising with Jesus in Everyday Life*

"As a quadriplegic living with chronic pain, I've wrestled through many battles against depression, resentment, envy of others, and fear of the future. Many things helped me overcome these skirmishes, but one, for sure, was the practical, sage advice of my friend, David Powlison. In his new book, *Safe and Sound: Standing Firm in Spiritual Battles*, David fits us with weapons of warfare that help the reader stand strong in Christ on the front lines of battle. I highly recommend this wonderful new book!"

Joni Eareckson Tada, Founder and CEO of Joni and Friends International Disability Center

"David helps us regain the language, perspective, and practice of spiritual warfare from the Scriptures. To counsel is to engage in cosmic battles waged in the normal moments of everyday life. Powlison keeps us grounded by reminding us that we do not wage war according to modern philosophies of naturalism, but with the armor of God and the Sword of the Spirit. In the midst of his own battles with the ever-present shadows of death, Powlison is transparent and vulnerable as he shepherds us to rest in the peace found in God's Word. Expositionally accurate, theologically practical, and winsomely relevant—you will do well to read, heed, and guard his timely biblical counsel."

T. Dale Johnson, Jr., Executive Director of the Association of Certified Biblical Counselors; Director of Counseling Programs at Midwestern Baptist Theological Seminary; Associate Professor of Biblical Counseling at Midwestern Baptist Theological Seminary

"What a gift David Powlison has given us in this, his final book. His familiar voice does what it has always done—it lovingly joins the dots of spiritual reality to the present reality of life. Hear him well: spiritual warfare is not an occasional oddity, it is the central dilemma of every person's life. This book doesn't just describe our constant battle—to believe, and repent, and love—it also shows us how to fight—right to the end. And no one who loved David, either in person or through his ministry, will read the final chapter without tears in their eyes."

Steve Midgley, Executive Director, Biblical Counselling UK; Senior Minister, Christ Church Cambridge

"I worked with David for thirty-eight years, so I acknowledge I am biased toward everything he wrote, but this is David at his best: pastoral, connecting dots between Ephesians and Satan's present strategies, opening his own life to us, and opening our eyes to the light of Jesus Christ. More than a book, this is a gift."

Edward T. Welch, Faculty and counselor, CCEF; author of *A Small Book about a Big Problem*

"Honestly I've always had more questions than answers when it comes to spiritual warfare and demonic activity. So I am thankful for this short, Scripture-saturated book that not only provides clear teaching on what spiritual warfare really is, but also presents appropriate strategies for helping people in the midst of spiritual battles against evil—the same strategies we all need for life in this world—the Word and prayer."

Nancy Guthrie, Author and Bible teacher

"This is the best thing I've ever read on spiritual warfare. David Powlison's *Safe and Sound* equipped me to understand spiritual warfare in a way that nothing else has before. Read it and I guarantee you'll grow in your faith."

Deepak Reju, Pastor of Biblical Counseling and Family Ministry, Capitol Hill Baptist Church (Washington, DC); author of *On Guard* and *She's Got the Wrong Guy*

SAFE AND SOUND

STANDING FIRM
IN SPIRITUAL BATTLES

David Powlison

New
Growth
Press

newgrowthpress.com

New Growth Press, Greensboro, NC 27404
newgrowthpress.com
Copyright © 2019 by David Powlison

Cover Design: Faceout Books, faceoutstudio.com
Interior Typesetting and eBook: lparnellbookservices.com

ISBN 978-1-948130-73-8 (Print)
ISBN 978-1-948130-83-7 (eBook)

Library of Congress Control Number: 2019908439

Printed in India

28 27 26 25 24 23 22 21   4 5 6 7 8

CONTENTS

INTRODUCTION

This is a book about spiritual warfare. You are in a battle. I am in a battle. And every person we counsel is—like us—living in a fog of war, stalked by a deadly predator, and facing a master of deception. When our hearts deceive us and our culture misleads us, Satan's desires and purposes are at work.

How does that strike you?

If you're like me, it can be hard to tell in the day-to-day that we are in this war. As with any spiritual reality, it's easy to forget when you can't see it with your own eyes. I wrote this book because I want us to be awake and alert to the real battles we face. These are dark days, and this is a book about how to stand up to the powers of darkness—for yourself, for your loved ones, for those you counsel. As we go forward, I am going to be personal. I will share stories with you to show what some battles have looked like in my life. I will share stories from other people's lives so we can benefit from what they've learned about how we are to stand. I will tell stories because this is not a topic that can stay abstract. The reality of The Great War for our souls is on the table in the Bible from Genesis 3 through Revelation 22. We are real people with a real problem. This is personal for all of us.

So to begin, let me go back to my beginnings.

~ ~ ~

For the first twenty-five years of my life I was unaware that I was in the middle of a battle with unseen forces. I grew up in a church in Hawaii that didn't believe in the devil and didn't have too much to say about Jesus either. We didn't actually need a savior because we weren't really sinners—at least not big ones. We thought of ourselves as basically good people with a few problems we could solve on our own. And we certainly didn't think or talk about the devil. But that didn't change the reality that I did have enemies: the world around me where we all lived without reference to God, my own desires that were ultimately self-focused, death and the shadow of death, and, over all, the dark lord Satan.

As a teenager I began to have a sense that I wasn't getting the whole picture of what life was about at my church. I could see that there was actual evil in the world. My dad was a Marine in the Pacific in World War II. After the war, we were faced with the threat of total destruction from the nuclear bomb. We had drills at school where we were all hiding under our desks in case a nuclear bomb was dropped. That was the world I was living in. It was a world where the religion that I grew up with seemed completely irrelevant.

By the time I was off to college at Harvard, I had given up any interest in religion. But my world continued to expand. Now my world included a campus in turmoil from student protests.

We protested against social injustice in Cambridge, against Harvard's rules and policies, and against the Vietnam War.

Death became real to me as well. My grandfather died when I was a freshman in college. I watched as he grappled with the meaning of his life in the face of death. He had no answers, and I had no answers to share with him. The next year I studied for a semester in France. One night I was in the backseat of a car when a young man, obviously drunk, stumbled right into our path. I looked him in the eye before the car hit him and he was killed. Once again, I met death and had no answers. What meaning could there be made out of a life that could end so suddenly and senselessly in death?

And there were my desires, thoughts, and intentions. I wanted to have significance, to understand people, to live a life that mattered, to care for others in some way, and have a relationship with a nice girl. To those ends I majored in psychology, brought water and bandages to those who were injured in riots, and practiced serial monogamy. Added to that was what I didn't want. I didn't want to be around Christians. I thought Christians were backward and reactionary. If I knew anyone who claimed to be a Christian, I kept as far away as possible.

I did have unanswered spiritual questions, but they weren't on the front burner of my life. After a few years in college, my worldview began to crack ever so slightly. God broke in through Bob Kramer, a friend I met at Harvard where we were both involved in protests together. He went to Europe for a year to study and ended up at L'Abri, where he met Francis Schaeffer and became a Christian. When he came back to college, it just so happened that we had space in our suite and he moved in with me.

That year Bob and I started a five-year conversation about Jesus. He was the first person I met who was thoughtful about his faith. He was able to mount an intellectual defense of Christianity that was very compelling, but the reason our conversation went on for five years is because I didn't want a savior. I didn't want a lord. I wanted to be in charge of my life and my choices. Our friendship endured—I was even his best man at his wedding to Diane—but I didn't change. I still didn't want to be a Christian.

But on August 31, 1975, something different happened. Our conversation started along the same lines with Bob explaining the philosophical and existential reasons for Christianity—which made perfect sense to me. Then Bob stopped making the case for Christianity and simply shared his heart with me. He said, "Diane and I really love you, and we respect you. But what you believe and how you're living . . . you are destroying yourself."

Bob had earned the right to say this to me, and the Spirit used those words in my life. I immediately came under an intense conviction of sin. My sins flashed before my eyes—attitudes, thoughts, and actions that just a few minutes before I had seen nothing wrong with. Most fundamental of all, it struck me that I had not believed in the love God had for me.

I just sat there. Bob had the guts and the wisdom to be quiet. Finally I said, "How do I become a Christian?" His response was funny because he started to talk apologetics again. I had to stop him and say, "No, no. I don't care about all that. What do I have to do to become a Christian?"

Then Bob shared God's promise of cleansing and a new heart from Ezekiel.

"I will sprinkle clean water on you, and you shall be clean from all your uncleannesses, and from all your idols I will cleanse you. And I will give you a new heart, and a new spirit I will put within you. And I will remove the heart of stone from your flesh and give you a heart of flesh." (Ezekiel 36:25–26)

This offer of cleansing, renewal, transformation—it was what I wanted and, for the first time, understood that I needed. But then, Satan, who all this time had been in the background of my life as the animating power behind the darkness and lies, spoke openly to me. The only way I can describe it is that I heard an evil voice. It wasn't my voice; it was a mocking, snarling, accusatory voice that was in direct competition with the promise of a new heart that Bob had just read to me. That voice was saying things like, "You're too unclean. You're hopeless. God could never accept you. If you went to Christ, you would pollute him."

I had a vivid sense of being caught in this battle between two voices, one of which was the voice of promise and hope, and one of which was the voice of darkness and hostility. It was the only time I've ever had an experience like that. But I was right on the cusp of leaving the kingdom of darkness, and the king of darkness was not letting me go without a fight.

I said to Bob, "I feel like I'm too bad to come to Christ. And I can't . . . I just can't ask God to change me." Bob said, "You can ask God for help to ask God into your heart. You can ask God for anything, so you could ask him for the strength to ask him to rescue you." So I did. My prayer was straight out of Luke 18, "God, be merciful to me, a sinner" (v. 13). I called to the Lord; the evil voice went away. My experience that night was right out of James 4:7–8. I drew near to God in repentance and faith, and the devil fled.

The next morning I woke up in a new universe. The world was full of light and brightness, and I was filled with torrents of joy. The first words that ran through my mind were, "I'm a Christian. I'm home." I was almost twenty-six, and I had the sense of having been on a hot, dusty road heading to nowhere for twenty-five years. Now I was where I really belonged.

This twenty-four-hour period was the first time I was aware that I was in a battle. I was facing powerful enemies—the world around me that ignored God and made fun of Christians, my desire to be my own savior and lord, and Satan, the animating power of all the lies I believe and the darkness I lived in. But God broke into my life. The Spirit used one friend who was willing to love me and tell me the truth about God, the world, and myself to bring light into my personal darkness.

In personal ministry, you will meet many people who, like me, have no idea that they are in the grip of the dark lord and his lies. When you are counseling people who do not yet know the Lord, then you know that they live within a fog of fundamental deception. They are disoriented to what life is about. They are walking in the dark and do not understand what they are stumbling over (Proverbs 4:19). You know that the deceiver of the whole world does not love his followers. He intends to kill them in the end—and so you must be prepared to offer help.

You will meet and help others who do know Christ. When you are counseling one of the Lord's beloved children, then you know that the devil bears a particular animosity toward this person. The great dragon, "that ancient serpent," is furious with "the woman and her offspring who keep the commandments of God and hold to the testimony of Jesus" (Revelation 12:9, 17). They were his once (Ephesians 2:3; 5:8). But they switched sides, turning from darkness to light, from death to life. But given their troubles and struggles, they have an essential need to know Christ as their refuge, protection, and strength—and so you must be prepared to offer help.

This book is about how to help people. Standing up to evil plunges us into deep, dark waters—the complexity of the human heart, the complexity of cultural influences, the complexity of the enemy. We must learn how to fight well, how to put on Jesus Christ himself, wearing the weapons of light with which he defeats the powers of darkness.

Together, let's stand up to the darkness in the pastoral wisdom of Christ Jesus himself!

Part 1: What Is Spiritual Warfare?

Chapter 1

THE REALITY OF SPIRITUAL WARFARE

Harry and Keisha are a couple in your church. Harry doesn't believe in Satan. He doesn't really believe in God either. In his world everything is up to him. There are no outside spiritual forces, just the choices that he makes. Right now he is choosing to have an affair and to leave Keisha, his wife of ten years. He wants you to give him permission to leave.

Joe meets with you and reports that his wife Laura believes that he has a demon of addiction causing him to drink too much. She often prays over him, casting out his demon. At first, he thought her prayers might have cured his drinking problem. His drinking was more under control. But lately things are pretty much the same. He still drinks too much. He wonders if he does have a demon of addiction and if maybe they just haven't found the right way to pray.

Kaitlin just became a Christian. She grew up in a Christian home where she was taught about Jesus but went her own way. She married and had three children and a year ago put her faith in Jesus. Now her husband Tom is adamantly opposed to her going to church and bringing the kids to church. She doesn't know what to do. She comes to you for guidance.

Stacey sees the devil's handiwork in every problem large and small. Once she cast out a demon from her computer. She was certain that a computer virus was the devil's work. When she describes a bad choice she has made, she always frames it as Satan getting the best of her. She really believes, in her words, "the devil made me do it."

~ ~ ~

If you were counseling Harry, Joe, Kaitlin, and Stacey, what would you say? Would you talk with them about the spiritual battle they are in and the unseen enemies they face? Or would you be more naturally drawn to talk about matters that are concrete and easier to describe: psychological dynamics, social influences, and physiological givens? How does the uncanny power of darkness fit in with the more accessible factors in a person's life? Is it possible that these seemingly accessible factors are actually far more elusive than we imagine, because they work hand in hand with the weaver of illusions and delusions?

Consider Harry who doesn't believe in God or Satan and yet is in the grip of Satan's lies about who he is actually serving and what brings true happiness. Can we fully understand his choices without some reference to how he is influenced by the lies that come to him from the world around him and his own desires—lies that originate from the dark lord? Or what about

Kaitlin. Can she really understand her husband's hatred of all things Christian without reference to the spiritual battle she is now in?

And then there is Stacey. Is she on to something when she makes the devil the "lead actor"? Would we be right to bring the devil into the conversation early and often, as if Satan's activity is the deepest and most significant explanation for everything that goes bad? Or perhaps Joe's wife, Laura, does well to see him as a "devil of the gaps," an extra factor, applicable only when a problem seems complex, bizarre, and particularly hard to solve.

How *do* we understand the role of the devil in the battles we are in?!

These are hard questions and it is so easy to go in the wrong direction when thinking about the role the Evil One plays in this world. In Part 1 of this book, we will see how Scripture helps us wisely answer these questions. Perhaps the fullest expression of how we are to stand against evil is in Ephesians 6:10–20, the classic passage on our participation in the clash between light and darkness. The engine room of this book will be unpacking that passage and trying on, piece by piece, the equipment God has given us for fighting evil. In Part 2, we will illustrate what spiritual warfare looks like in real life with case studies of people facing different battles.

Let's begin with how the Bible leads us to think about spiritual warfare.

THINKING BIBLICALLY ABOUT SPIRITUAL WARFARE

Did you know that the term *spiritual warfare* never appears in Scripture? It is a pastoral-theological term describing the conflict occurring at the heart of the Christian life. For good, biblical, and practical reasons, Christians have always understood that we face a three-fold moral enemy: the world, the flesh, and the devil. Over this unholy trinity hangs the specter of our last enemy—the shadow of death and death itself. Scripture teaches that all of these enemies are ruled by Satan, the prince of this world.

Even though the term doesn't appear in Scripture, here are four ways to understand spiritual warfare biblically. I will make comments after each.

First, *spiritual warfare is a metaphor for standing on the Lord's side in the epic struggle between the Lord and his enemies.* Your counselees are taking sides. Your aim as a Christian pastor, counselor, and friend is to protect children of light (Ephesians 5:8) from being wooed back into darkness and to woo the rest of mankind (Ephesians 2:3) out of darkness and into the light.

Second, *spiritual warfare is a moral struggle.* It is a conflict over who you are, what you believe, and how you live. Our sufferings, whatever their form or cause—and Satan's malice is in the mix of causes—provide occasions either to stumble into darkness or to stand in the light. Our warfare is over which it will be. So, for example, Satan instigated the deaths of Job's children, the loss of his wealth, the disease that wracked his body, and his wife's evil counsel. But, ultimately, the spiritual warfare was for the loyalty of Job's soul. He had to make a moral choice: Who will he serve? Who will be his Shepherd?

Elsewhere in Scripture, the book of James focuses on the moral struggle within the heart. James zeroes in on two drives of the human heart: "I am" and "I want" (James 3:13—4:12). He takes the example of interpersonal conflict and shows how the self-exalting "I am god" leads to "I want my way." And, "No matter the cost to others, it's my will that needs to be done." James emphasizes how Satan interacts with our own hearts, what James calls "the flesh." Satan's lies and distortions are part of the mix, but repentance and humility before God will cause him to flee (James 4:7). His searching indictment of the human heart ends with the call to submit to God, resist the devil, and humble your heart.

Third, *spiritual warfare is a synonym for the struggles of the Christian life.* There are no special insights or special techniques that kick in just because Satan's fingerprints are on something that is happening. It's all one war—and his mark is on every struggle that is wrong and dark.

Fourth, *spiritual warfare is a battle for lordship.* At its core, it's the battle for who you will serve. In whose image are you being made? Will you resemble the good Shepherd who lays down his life for his sheep? Or will you grow more and more like Satan, the liar and destroyer? This is a battle that encompasses all of life. Not just for a few odd or bizarre moments, but in every moment of every day we are in a battle for who we will serve.

In summary, Scripture treats spiritual warfare as a normal, everyday part of the Christian life, and so we should as well. It's not about spooky special effects. It's about how we think, feel, live, desire, and act in the presence of our enemies. The ultimate question that runs through everyone's life and through the whole Bible is: Who will be your shepherd? Will you be shepherded by your good heavenly Father or by *the* liar and murderer—Satan?

Christians are often confused about what role Satan actually does play in the world and in our own lives in particular. But God's Word gives clarity and direction. So let's look more closely at our enemy and what he is up to.

THE REALITY OF SATAN

The Bible never ignores Satan and the forces of evil arrayed against God's people. The Evil One is not the primary actor, but he does not only appear when something unusually strange or evil is going on. The real devil is utterly normal, and his role is fully integrated into daily life. Mundane evil is the devil's business.

At the same time, Scripture never puts Satan and his activities front and center. God puts people and our relationship to him and each other front and center. Then, just often enough, so you don't forget, he lifts the curtain and says, "By the way—" and gives you a glimpse of what's happening backstage.

Jesus gives us one of the clearest descriptions of who Satan is and what he is doing in John 8 as he speaks to the religious leaders who have rejected him.

> "Why do you not understand what I say? It is because you cannot bear to hear my word. You are of your father the devil, and your will is to do your father's desires. He was a murderer from the beginning, and does not stand in the truth, because there is no truth in him. When he lies, he speaks out of his own character, for he is a liar and the father of lies." (John 8:43–44)

This passage encapsulates the core aspects of Satan's identity and purposes and works and motivations and intentions. Satan is intentionally evil, and he is up to no good. He has desires he wants us to follow. He is a father. He raises children. He disciples his children in evil. Jesus points out that this is nothing new. He traces Satan's lies all the way back to Genesis 3 where the serpent's lies led to death for the human race.

When the apostle John discusses the interplay of flesh, world, and devil throughout his first letter, he sums up the problem in one pithy sentence: "The whole world lies in the power of the evil one" (1 John 5:19). John is not being spooky or seeing a devil behind every bush. As we've seen, human life is defined by the struggle between light and darkness, good and evil, true and false, life and death. The devil sums up all that is dark, evil, false, and deadly.

Similarly, the apostle Paul discusses the same interplay of evils throughout his writing, and most pointedly in Ephesians 2:1–3:

> You were dead in the trespasses and sins in which you once walked, following the course of this world, following the prince of the power of the air, the spirit that is now at work in the sons of disobedience—among whom we all once lived in the passions of our flesh, carrying out the desires of the body and the mind, and were by nature children of wrath, like the rest of mankind.

Peter takes up Jesus's theme of Satan as murderer in 1 Peter where he describes the work of Satan as oriented around the experiences of suffering and oppression from outside forces. The issue of moral likeness is also there, but the context is how to remain faithful as you are faced with his murderous threats and intentions. Peter is emphasizing how Satan is in the world as a roaring lion seeking to devour God's people and destroy their faith by brute force (1 Peter 5:8).

Taking all of these passages together, we see that the devil plays an underlying, behind-the-scenes role in the everyday problems of sin, misery, and death. But, again, the Bible does not lead us to make the liar and murderer the focus of ministry.

People and their relationship with God are the focus. So, do speak of the devil, but don't talk too much. The way you pay attention to Satan is analogous to how you pay attention to other influencing factors: bodily problems, personal history, cultural and peer influences, situational stressors, and sufferings. They are in the mix, but the person as a moral responder always comes front and center.

We will now go deeper with Ephesians. In his letter, Paul emphasizes Satan's work in the world through schemes and lies and gives us direction on how to stand against Satan's lies. As we will see, this is not just a defensive posture. This is a call to active resistance.

Chapter 2

HOW PAUL ENVISIONS
SPIRITUAL WARFARE

As image-bearers of God, we all have an imaginative capacity. When we think about a coming event, we have a whole set of associations that help us envision what that will be like. Take, for example, when snow is predicted. Depending on your point of view, how you envision that event will vary. Some people envision a problem, a hassle—a struggle to shovel, to get the car out, to get to work. Children usually envision a snow storm quite differently. They are excited and happy—no school, sleeping in, sledding. I grew up in Hawaii and so I envision a snowstorm as a special treat—one of life's great joys.

In a similar way, how we envision spiritual warfare will affect how we think about our lives as Christians. It will affect how you seek to help and counsel others. Some Christians envision spiritual warfare as a scary movie with ghosts and bizarre special effects. Others don't envision the battle we are in at all. They don't live in the reality that we are up against forces bigger than ourselves, forces that are highly deceptive, and are vying for our allegiance.

Paul, in Ephesians, provides the counterpoint to fear and to indifference. In the previous chapter, we saw four ways the Bible helps us understand spiritual warfare. To build upon that understanding, we will here hone in on four key truths Paul offers us about how to envision spiritual warfare. These truths will clear up our misconceptions about spiritual warfare and the role of the armor of God. Then we will look at how "be strong in the Lord and in the strength of his might" is the overarching theme of all of Ephesians, including the section on spiritual warfare.

Here is Ephesians 6:10–20, the passage we will work with over these next two chapters:

[10] Finally, be strong in the Lord and in the strength of his might. [11] Put on the whole armor of God, that you may be able to stand against the schemes of the devil. [12] For we do not wrestle against flesh and blood, but against the rulers, against the authorities, against the cosmic powers over this present darkness, against the spiritual forces of evil in the heavenly places. [13] Therefore take up the whole armor of God, that you may be able to withstand in the evil day, and having done all, to stand firm. [14] Stand therefore, having fastened on the belt of truth, and having put on the breastplate of righteousness, [15] and, as shoes for your feet, having put on the readiness given by the gospel of peace. [16] In all circumstances take up the shield of faith, with which you can extinguish all the flaming darts of the evil one; [17] and take the helmet of salvation, and the sword of the Spirit, which is the word of God, [18] praying at all times in the Spirit, with all prayer and supplication. To that

end, keep alert with all perseverance, making supplication for all the saints, [19] and also for me, that words may be given to me in opening my mouth boldly to proclaim the mystery of the gospel, [20] for which I am an ambassador in chains, that I may declare it boldly, as I ought to speak.

First, it is important to remember that Ephesians 6:10–20 is not introducing a new topic. Paul begins this section by saying "finally" and that's our signal that he is giving a summary of his letter. This passage draws together everything that Paul has already been saying, and puts an exclamation point on it. Here are six key elements that thread through the whole letter and simply come to a climax in this conclusion.

- Jesus Christ is the Lord. Throughout Ephesians, Paul shows how God's grace has brought us into his Son's mercy, power, and mission. At the center of spiritual warfare is not the devil. It's Jesus Christ.
- God is powerful and merciful. Paul has repeatedly affirmed the life-giving strength of God working within us (1:19; 2:5, 10; 3:16–20).
- The spiritual forces of evil—devil, flesh, world—are active. Paul has already brought in what we might call this dark trinity of evil throughout the letter and how they work in synergy with each other. He has already described the cosmic authorities (1:21; 3:10), the deadly hold of the world, the evil and darkness of fallen hearts (2:1–3; 4:17–19), and our call to stand against the devil's purposes (4:27).
- We live in difficult times. Paul has previously called us to be alert and wise when the days are dark (4:14; 5:3–17).

- We are to walk as children of light. Ephesians has already spoken in great detail about how faith, love, and wisdom (1:12–19; 2:8–10; 3:14–6:9) supplant foolishness, alienation, and hardness of heart (2:1–3; 2:11–13; 4:14; 4:17–5:18). At the heart of Ephesians as a whole is the battle for the loyalty of our hearts. Do we walk as children of light or children of darkness? Whose voice do we listen to? What will shape our choices and our relationships? These are the crucial questions that Paul is focusing on throughout Ephesians.
- Pray for others. Paul has already given vivid, first-person examples of how to intercede for each other about what we most need (1:16–23; 3:14–21).

All of Ephesians is about our conflict with darkness—within ourselves, with other people, with the spiritual forces of evil. Christ's triumph over all that is evil, dark, and deadly is the message throughout. Now all these strands come together in one final description of life in Christ. Spiritual warfare is our participation in the Lord's cosmic war with darkness. The Lord is the warrior. The weapons describe his strength and what he does. By his strength we participate in what he is doing. Ephesians 6:10–20 shows us how. Ephesians 6 is not changing the subject. Failure to recognize that turns "spiritual warfare" into a wildcard of ideas and practices that are antithetical to the Lord's explicit teaching and intentions.

Second, it's important to remember that spiritual warfare is done together, as the body of Christ. The whole of Ephesians is about the body of Christ, and Paul is not suddenly switching focus in the section on the armor of God. A friend of mine put it this way: "We don't want to envision a whole bunch of little individuals running around in armor." Instead, envision the body of Christ standing in battle together.

We each do our part, so we are not negating the individual, but we are doing our parts together as one body. When Paul says in Ephesians 4:27 not to give the devil a foothold, he is referring to divisions within the body of Christ. Ephesians is about union and communion with Christ and union and communion with each other in Christ. Spiritual warfare is against the forces that would divide and break our fellowship with Christ and with one another.

Spiritual warfare is not just about ourselves and our relationship with God. It's about the people around us. Who benefits when we stand against the world, the flesh, and the devil? Yes, God is glorified when we stand. Yes, we are blessed when we stand. But other people also benefit. When we live as children of light, the light of the glory of God shines in our dark world. Standing against evil is not a separate topic from the one-anothering passages in Ephesians 4 and 5. We stand against evil and shine light into darkness as we live out Paul's call to "Be kind to one another, tenderhearted, forgiving one another, as God in Christ forgave you" (Ephesians 4:32).

Third, it is important that we rightly envision the "panoplion" of God. The word *panoplion* is usually translated "whole armor." But "armor" creates the wrong mental picture, and popular teaching on this passage puts the emphasis in the wrong places. For starters, panoplion does not mean protective armor. It means the "complete weaponry" needed to go into combat. It means you have all the tools to do the job. You are fully outfitted and equipped for a calling. Paul chose this metaphor to give us a striking mental picture, but he is not commenting on the outfit worn by Roman soldiers (as the metaphor is frequently explained). His images come from Isaiah and the Psalms. The soldier we are to imagine is not a Roman centurion, but the divine, messianic King of kings. We are to imagine the LORD God coming in person, coming in power, coming to make right all that is wrong.

Fourth, it is important that we rightly envision spiritual warfare as mounting an offense, not playing defense. Popular teaching makes associations about the protective aspect of individual items. But the Bible uses this imagery to portray the Lord overthrowing the powers-that-be in a darkened world. Christ comes bringing mercy to the humble and mayhem to the haughty. Paul is not describing how to maintain a defensive posture. When the Lord comes in person, he is taking initiative. He is not on the defensive.

Spiritual warfare is what happens when he enlists us in his cause and equips us to join his battle. It's about light invading darkness. Often when people envision spiritual warfare, they think "I'm under attack" and that is true. Satan does have his wily ways and he is out to get us. But we are also God's invading army, and we are on the attack. We are bringing light into a dark world. The children of light, the army of light, the servants of light are on the offensive.

In 2 Corinthians, Paul references all of his hardships, but then talks about how he has the "weapons of righteousness in the right hand and the left" (2 Corinthians 6:7 NIV). Paul is going to war. The war is not just coming to him. But what are the weapons he fights with? They are humility, love, truth, courage, faithfulness, goodness, and wisdom. These are unusual weapons, aren't they? It's much easier to rely on special words or prayers that will cast out demons. But the real project of spiritual warfare is much harder and much better. We fight like Jesus did when he came to this dark world. He is the Lord of light and he calls us to bring the light of his love into this dark world.

THE STRENGTH OF GOD

Now let's look at how the Lord's strength and purposes are embodied in his complete weaponry. Ephesians 6:10 is the main teaching point of the entire passage: "Finally, be strong in the Lord and in the strength of his might." You need Christ's strength. Paul introduces the weaponry metaphor in the sentences that follow in order to put a sharp point on our need for strength from outside ourselves—strength that the Lord freely gives. His merciful power raised Christ and is now working in you (1:17–19). His power joined you to Christ, remaking you for good works (2:5–10). His power made Paul a minister to all nations (3:7–10). His power strengthens you in your inner being (3:16–21).

The point of Ephesians 1–3 is Christ's strength for us and in us. The point of Ephesians 4–6 is how to live a worthwhile life by his strength. Paul closes his letter by strongly reminding us that the Lord's strength is the only basis for goodness. He gives strength for us to go out and live the Christian life. Spiritual warfare means finding strength to live a life of faith, humility, love, goodness, courage, and wisdom. It means facing all the darkly evil forces that mightily oppose such things. It means strength for us to live our lives with the same merciful purposes as Christ. It means strength to forgive others as God in Christ forgave us. It means strength for us to walk in love as he loved us and gave himself for us. This is our walk and warfare. This is Christ's call to you. And this is his call to the men, women, and children whom you befriend, mentor, disciple, and counsel.

Ephesians 6:10 ties up the entire letter. Then Paul drives the point home with a powerful image. Because the Lord of hosts is at war with the darkness, you also are at war. You were darkness, but now you are light, so walk as a child of the light.

God's strength is the complete weaponry of light (Ephesians 6:11–13; cf. Romans 13:12–14). Each component of his strength equips you to join the fight (Ephesians 6:14–17). The powers of wrong are strong. The wreckage of human life bears dreadful witness (2:1–3; 4:17–19, 22). But in the end the wrong and false will be undone by the power and truth of God. Through Christ, God's strength will triumph over all the dark rulers, authorities, cosmic powers, and spiritual forces of evil. In the end, we will stand with him and they will all fall.

Chapter 3

GOD'S WEAPONS
AND GOD'S CALL

Now that we have learned to envision spiritual warfare as an everyday part of every Christian's life where we are equipped by Christ to fight evil, we are ready to look more closely at each piece of weaponry. When we examine it piece by piece and consider Paul's biblical sources, we get a coherent picture of what God is calling us into. Spiritual warfare is about taking the battle *to* the darkness, with the Lord as our strength and protection. The first four items are part of one long sentence that calls us to stand up to the power of evil.

Therefore, stand, having fastened on the belt of truth (6:14a). This is an interesting place for Paul to start, because the truth that is in Jesus, which Paul has been speaking of all through Ephesians, is completely outside of human experience and human imagination. No one could have made this up. It's too good to be true—Christ died for sinners! Christ is raised to life by the power of God. We have life in him. We are raised with him. God dwells with his people. At the very core of Ephesians is the revelation of Jesus Christ, and it is this revelation that holds everything together. We gird ourselves with Christ. Just like a belt holds us together, so the truth of who Christ is and his saving work hold us together. This Christ who was crushed and humbled unto death, even death on a cross, has triumphed over sin, death, and the grave. The belt of truth must come first. If Christ is not raised, then faith is futile, we are still in our sins, and the darkness wins. But if Christ is true, then all the old rules and rulers are overthrown. Death and moral darkness lose. All that is wrong will become untrue. Christ is true. And by speaking truth in love, we grow up (4:15).

Where did Paul get his image of a belt? He took it directly from Isaiah 11:5. Isaiah 11–12 is a messianic promise, followed by songs of joy when the promise comes true. The Savior will arise from the lineage of David. He will be filled with the Holy Spirit of wisdom beyond measure. He will invade the earth where predators now cause pain and death. He is not on the defensive. He will bring justice and mercy for the meek, and destruction to the godless. We recognize Jesus Christ as the man who fastened on the belt of truth. Isaiah's words are now fulfilled.

By nature and nurture, you and those you counsel have lie-darkened and lie-calloused hearts. In Ephesians, the primary lens on Satan is the liar who would seduce us and master us with his lies. Paul singles out the lies of the world, the lies of the devil, and the lies of our own hearts and counters them all with the truth of the gospel. These lies are always untruths about God, ourselves, and others. As you speak with others, you can help them identify those lies and see them for what they are—an attempt by Satan to disciple us in his image. But we are being remade in the image of Christ. We, too, can fasten on the belt of truth, and be filled with the Spirit of wisdom. You and those you counsel can stand in the truth. You and those you counsel can gird yourself with truth and turn from the lies of the world, the flesh, and the devil. Putting on the belt of truth means depending every day on Christ. He is the way, the truth, and the life.

Therefore, stand, having put on the breastplate of righteousness (6:14b). Often we imagine that the breastplate of righteousness is only defensive and protective. The righteousness of Christ does protect our core. Because Christ's righteousness is now ours, we are protected from the death that we deserve for our sins. But Paul also wants us to envision Christ's righteousness in action. He is describing the goodness, love, faith, and humility that Jesus lived while here on earth. The same righteousness that is now ours must express itself in how we treat others. It protects us because it's the opposite of hate and pride and unbelief—which tears us and others apart.

Throughout Ephesians Paul calls us to the simple beauty of righteousness. "Walk as children of light (for the fruit of light is found in all that is good and right and true), and try to discern what is pleasing to the Lord" (Ephesians 5:8–10). Righteousness is the way to take on all that is hurtful and false. Christ's battle strategy is to do what is right and good, and to say what is true and helpful.

Paul received this image from Isaiah 59:17. Who arms himself in this way? Isaiah 59:1–21 makes it clear: the Lord God comes to earth wearing the breastplate of righteousness. He alone can make right all that is so wrong. Isaiah 59 describes a grim world where darkness and sin reign. Everything is turned upside down. The Lord's people groan in misery and despair. No one on the scene can turn things around. Then the Lord comes in person. He comes in wrath and mercy. He brings justice to destroy his enemies while pouring out grace—his Spirit, words, and redeeming mercies—on those who turn from transgression. He is on an offensive. Only when wrenched out of its divine, missional context does this military hardware seem to be defensive armor. The weaponry is embodied in a person on a mission. The word picture describes Jesus Christ in action.

Seeing him, we stand up, do what is right, and say what is constructive. We join Jesus's mission. We entreat our counselees to join Jesus's mission. We remind them that any glass of cold water is an act of righteousness, any word that is constructive, not destructive, any word that is true, not false, any word that builds bridges instead of creates distance. These might seem small and insignificant, but, in God's kingdom, their impact is huge. Any act of goodness builds the communion of saints. It builds relationship. It's a righteousness that pushes back the kingdom of darkness, evil, unkindness, and hate—and fills the world with the light of God's love.

Therefore, stand, having put on as shoes for your feet the readiness given by the gospel of peace (6:15). The gospel of peace—reconciling Jews and Gentiles to God and to each other—is a central theme in Ephesians 2–3. In the gospel of peace, relationships are reconciled, forgiveness triumphs over anger, and a community of mutual kindness is established. This came through powerfully in Ephesians 4:25–5:2. The gospel embodies peace-making power.

Where did Paul find this picture? It is a rich allusion to Isaiah 52:7:

> How beautiful upon the mountains are the feet of him
> who brings good news,
> who publishes peace,
> who brings good news of happiness,
> who publishes salvation,
> who says to Zion, "Your God reigns."

Whose feet are beautiful with the good news of peace? Isaiah 52:6–10 makes clear that the shoes belong to the Lord who is coming in person: "It is I who speak. Here I am." Every eye sees the Lord returning to Zion, bringing comfort and redemption. A few sentences later, Isaiah 53 will tell us how he will do it. The Lamb of God will bear the iniquity of us all. Paul writes Ephesians looking back both at Isaiah and at Jesus Christ, that Lamb of God whom death could not hold. He came to save and to reign.

Jesus Christ *is* the good news of peace to the ends of the earth. The man wearing these shoes is on the march. Stand up and join him. Those you counsel need good news. Their hearing, their healing, makes them bearers of good news.

Therefore, stand, in all circumstances having taken up the shield of faith, with which you can extinguish all the flaming darts of the evil one (6:16). We are on the march, but the enemy fights back—hard. He lies, he schemes, he accuses, he hurts, he divides. He would enslave you and kill you, if he could. Ephesians has reminded us that wherever lies and hostility control a relationship, the devil dominates (4:25–27). We are to stand against the devil's purposes and plans (6:11).

The shield is the one piece of weaponry that Paul did not pull from Isaiah. It is the only piece that intends to communicate a protective role as we face counterattacks of lies and hostilities. In every life circumstance, our shield repels "the flaming darts of the evil one." Where does the shield image come from? The Psalms are the source of this imagery. What is the shield? The Lord himself is a shield to those who take refuge in him when faced with enemies. In numerous psalms, our enemies are characterized as liars and murderers. They hate the Lord and his people. They are the devil's earthly image-bearers.

Psalm 18 is an example of faith seeking protection and strength in the Lord. In the first few verses David piles up every safe-place metaphor he can think of. This is what it looks like when a person takes up the shield of faith:

> I love you, O LORD, my strength.
> The LORD is my rock and my fortress and my deliverer,
>   my God, my rock, in whom I take refuge,
>   my shield, and the horn of my salvation, my stronghold.
> I call upon the LORD, who is worthy to be praised,
>   and I am saved from my enemies.

Notice, the LORD *is* the shield. Faith *per se* has no protective power. But faith looks with confidence to the one who protects and strengthens. This is how Christ took up the shield. This is how we, who are in Christ, continue to abide in Christ and strengthen ourselves in him.

Notice one more detail. The Messiah says these words at the opening of Psalm 18 as he is heading out to war. He will be both shielded (18:30–31, 35) and strengthened to pursue his enemies (18:29, 32–42). Even the "defensive" weapon of Ephesians 6 is portrayed as an aspect of the divine pursuit that defeats evil. Of course, spiritual warfare means you face fierce counterattacks from the darkness, but light is always taking initiative. Like you, your counselees are beset with weakness and darkness. And like you, they are called to actively push against evil. The Lord goes before us in our battle with all that bedevils us.

Take hold of the helmet of salvation (6:17a). Paul starts a new sentence for the final two pieces of equipment. We've been getting prepared. Now fully dressed and equipped, we grab our helmet and sword and head out into action. We are bringing a message of salvation to people who are dead, adrift, darkened and deviant, without God, and without hope. And these are not just words on paper. Christ is our salvation from death and sin. Salvation! A Savior! He comes in person for people who have lost their way and are dying. He came for us, and we go forth for others. We are living the message, wearing this helmet of salvation. Paul has spoken about this Gift of gifts throughout his letter. What was that truth with which we first girded ourselves as we sought the Lord's strength?

> When you heard the word of truth, the gospel of your salvation, and believed in him, you were sealed with the promised Holy Spirit. (Ephesians 1:13)

And what was that breastplate, footgear, and shield? It is the reality that Jesus Christ saves us from death, depravity, and the devil.

> When we were dead in our trespasses, [he] made us alive together with Christ—by grace you have been saved. (Ephesians 2:5)

We were dead, and the Spirit made us alive. He awakened faith by his power. The Lord freely gifts all good, and we gratefully receive. Your counselees need the encouragement of their salvation. The saving love of Christ is the only imperishable, incorruptible, and unfading hope. Counseling as *ministry* encourages, inspires, and motivates people with the truth of God's saving grace.

Paul returned to Isaiah for this piece of equipment. In fact, the helmet is the companion to the breastplate of righteousness in Isaiah 59:17. Everything we said a few paragraphs earlier applies again. Let me remind you that Isaiah 59:2–15 is bleak. The power of this present darkness is fully evident. The people of God are overwhelmed by their own evils. They feel their helplessness to change. The Lord must come in person. He must come to save us, or all is lost. So he comes as a warrior of salvation.

Why did Paul separate the breastplate and the helmet, the two halves of Isaiah 59:17, as he unpacked the weaponry of righteousness? I suspect that the answer does not lie in trying to find some intrinsic logic in how an assemblage of weapons works. The logic emerges because Paul is steeped in all that the Lord has promised in Christ. To be saved from death is the sum of all blessing. Isaiah 59 ties together all the threads of this great salvation. The LORD says,

> "This is my covenant with them: my Spirit that is upon you, and my words that I have put in your mouth, shall not depart out of your mouth, or out of the mouth of your offspring, or out of the mouth of your children's offspring . . . from this time forth and forevermore." (v. 21)

The gift of the new covenant in the coming of Christ our Savior, and the gift of the life-giving Spirit, and the gift of words of salvation—this is Ephesians. This is the light that we bring against the darkness.

The final piece of weaponry will now connect the Holy Spirit to God's lifesaving words about Christ.

Take the sword of the Spirit, which is the Word of God (6:17b). The Bible often fills out a metaphor from multiple angles. As we listen, as we stop and think, we get the point. Remember how those first few lines of Psalm 18 piled up ten straight word pictures for strength and safety, ten ways the Lord is "my ___"! Paul is doing the same sort of thing in Ephesians 6 as he piles up pictures of Christ's strong weapons of lifesaving war. What we've seen in Ephesians 6 are different ways of saying the same thing—how you strengthen yourself in the Lord, how you walk in the light, how you respond to the word of truth. He wants us to get the point.

This final piece of weaponry is another allusion to Isaiah. Isaiah 49:2 provides the most obvious reference to a weapon of divine words. These are words of the servant of the Lord, the Messiah, who says, "He made my mouth like a sharp sword." This sword expresses the wisdom of the Spirit, destroying evil and bringing in the peaceable kingdom. Isaiah 49:1–13 (like Isaiah 11, discussed earlier) proclaims the light of life to the whole earth. It identifies a man whom the Lord calls by name from his mother's womb. He will be glorified. By what he does, the Lord will be glorified. Before that, however, his life appears to come to nothing, because he is despised and rejected by his own people. But in the end, he will prove to be their Redeemer. More than that, he will be a Savior for all nations. Again, we recognize the biography of Jesus Christ. We are now invited to take up this sword of the Spirit and proclaim the one who was made "a light to the nations, that my salvation may reach to the end of the earth" (49:6). Strengthen yourself in this Lord, and go where the darkness reigns.

How do we proclaim Jesus in the Word as we counsel others? Just as a sermon is not simply a patchwork of Bible quotes, neither is a good counseling session just sharing a few Bible verses and sending counselees on their way. As you share the Word of God, you need the keen edge of wisdom that the metaphor "sword" brings to mind. Our words to those we minister to should be true to the Scripture, but also inhabit and address their current situation.

Often counselees have already heard Scripture applied to their current situation. But they are sitting in front of you because this hasn't "worked" for them. They have listened to sermons, gone to Bible studies, read the Bible, and listened to worship music, but nothing is clicking. If you start by simply pointing to all of these good things, you will be talking past the person in front of you.

That doesn't mean we should shy away from using the Bible in our counseling. We should be speaking truth from God's Word into the lives of counselees—sometimes with direct quotes, sometimes with a paraphrase of Scripture, but always taking care to wrap their struggles in the Word of God and in the belt of truth that is Jesus Christ. And always with a listening ear for what they are facing and how the Spirit is at work in them and through them.

Often I will ask someone, "What has been the passage that most turned on the lights for you, that changed your life, that brought you to faith?" Almost without fail what a person is struggling with right now—perhaps ten, twenty, or thirty years later—is some further extension and application of what first awakened faith. As someone shares how the Word has helped in the past, that becomes a way for you to connect the dots between current life experience and Scripture. Your conversation can build on what the Spirit has already done and how it is freshly relevant to the struggles today.

Take up the helmet and the sword, *praying at all times in the Spirit, with all prayer and supplication, to that end, keeping alert with all perseverance, making supplication for all the saints* (6:18). Paul has described six weapons of the Lord's strength. Now he has finished using the weaponry metaphor but he continues unpacking our need to seek strength and aid. The Holy Spirit's present power is the focus. The animating author of the Word is also the animating author of our faith. Faith responds to God's truth by interceding for the real needs of others. Paul had prayed for us to know the Lord's strength, love, and presence (1:16–23; 3:14–21). He called each of us to find strength in the Lord (6:10) and to take refuge in the Lord (6:16). Now, personal need moves to concern for the needs of others. Faith cascades into love. We pray for our fellow saints who have the same need for the Lord's truth, strength, love, presence, and protection. When you counsel others, they need your prayers for strength in the Lord. And the people they love need the same care from them. The personal conversations of counseling are one form of "prayer and the ministry of the Word" (Acts 6:4). We are about the work of awakening others to reality so they can stand up to the darkness.

What Paul says next is astonishing. He has called us to pray for each other. Now he puts himself first in the queue of needy ones:

> making supplication . . . also for me, that words may be given to me in opening my mouth boldly to proclaim the mystery of the gospel, for which I am an ambassador in chains, that I may declare it boldly, as I ought to speak. (6:18–20)

He needed our Lord's help as much as you do.

One of the great charms of Christian truth is that we have a faith of equal standing with the great apostles (2 Peter 1:1), and that great apostles have needs of equal urgency with ours. Paul is our brother. He needed the prayers of the Ephesians so he would be strengthened to take up the sword of the Spirit and speak words of life. Just as he had prayed that their faith would be deepened by gifts of the Spirit, he needed the same prayers from them. He, too, needed the weaponry of strength to enable him to engage in Christ's mission—this belt, breastplate, shoes, shield, helmet, and sword of life that invades darkness with truth, faith, and love. You and your counselees have a faith of equal standing and needs of equal urgency.

We have come full circle. We have looked at how the big picture in Ephesians informs our understanding of Christ's warfare with evil, and we have unpacked this spectacular vision of the weaponry. Now we will move to Part 2 and consider how to walk out the implications in the struggles and battles of everyday life.

Part 2: Counseling in the Reality of Spiritual Warfare

Chapter 4

STRENGTH AND GUIDANCE
FOR PERSONAL MINISTRY

A clear view of what Ephesians 6 teaches fills us with hope for ourselves and others. Yes, we are in a battle, but we are equipped with Christ himself. But as we struggle in this world and come alongside fellow strugglers, some of that confidence can dissipate as we face real problems in a painful world. I have sought to capture the energy, initiative, and activity of Christ's warfare, as Scripture portrays it. But that raises an existential problem. Life is often hard and ugly. The Evil One animates incalculable evils. These are dark days. It is easy to feel overwhelmed, besieged, threatened, and vulnerable. This is perhaps why more defensive descriptions of spiritual warfare have been typical.

With so much light, life, truth, goodness, strength, and protection pouring forth from Christ, why is the process so messy? Why are churches so weak and compromised? Why do we stumble so often? Why do we have so many blind spots?

Ephesians 6 is energetic and courageous, but it is also realistic. Paul underscores the powers of evil. He reminds us that the days are evil so we won't be surprised when the clash between light and darkness takes place in our own hearts, our own families, our own churches. He reminds us so we aren't thrown off by the confusing fog of war and the fact that we take hits.

Paul talks at the highest level about the forces of wickedness. This in itself can be helpful. It helps to know that our deepest enemies are not flesh and blood—especially when we, children of light, relapse into fighting with each other or retaliating against people who attack from outside. It helps us to "lower the temperature" when we face human conflicts. But Paul is not naïve about what happens in and among people: the church's many failures, the stubbornness of our sin, and the grievousness of suffering. After all, he wrote letters to the Corinthians and Galatians! But Ephesians doesn't go into the gritty particulars of the struggle, except to remind us of what we once were.[1] Ephesians is our call to be different, not a description of how what we once were is all too often what we still are. This particular letter takes the high view of what Christ has done for us and what his Spirit is doing in us. When the battle is finally won, when we have done all and are standing, then this high call will be fully realized. Meanwhile, to better understand how the struggle actually thinks, feels, and wrestles, we have Job, Psalms, Proverbs, Ecclesiastes, and many other parts of the New Testament.

TWO ROLE MODELS FOR OUR SPIRITUAL BATTLE

We can also be encouraged that, right in Ephesians, we have not one, but two role models. As we have discussed, the weaponry

---

1. See Ephesians 2:1–2, 12–13; 4:17–22; and all the negatives in 4:25–5:18.

of God describes the Lord himself on mission, wearing and embodying his own weapons. In his life, death, and resurrection, Jesus triumphed over the powers of darkness. He knew the ugly reality of the world, the flesh, and the devil better than any human before or since. In the midst of his real enemies, he trusted in his heavenly Father to bring light out of darkness. He continually called those he encountered to that same living, active dependence on his heavenly Father.

Jesus recognizes that the Evil One plays a consequential role in forming the characteristics of human defection and misery. But he continually speaks to the human heart. In John 8 when Jesus describes the devil, he is speaking to the people in front of him (John 8:44–47). The devil is significant, but he is directly posing questions about life or death to his listeners. These are the same questions we are to ask of ourselves and others:

- Who is fathering you?
- Whose words are catching your ear?
- Whose desires are you following?
- Who do you say I am?

Everything you see and hear in other people's lives, and everything you say and do in counseling is downstream from how you and they are answering these definitive questions.

We also have another role model. In the pages of Ephesians, Paul has already been doing everything he tells us to do. We witness Paul living out spiritual warfare. The entire letter is a self-disclosure of Paul's assault on darkness wearing the weaponry of light.

As we read this letter, we are witnesses to how Paul also continually speaks to the human heart. He wears the belt, speaking truth in love with constructive, timely, and grace-giving words.

He wears the breastplate of righteousness, a living demonstration of a man redeemed by grace and living fruitfully as God's workmanship. His feet walk in the gospel of peace, reconciling people with God and once-estranged peoples with each other. Paul takes up the shield of faith, audibly seeking the God of power and strength. He wears the helmet of salvation: his message, his ministry, his incandescent awareness of Jesus our Savior. And, of course, Paul is taking up the Word of God in the power of the Spirit. Ephesians *is* the Word of God and it is brimming with the Spirit's presence! And throughout Ephesians, Paul continually cites and applies other Scriptures in ways that are both faithful and fresh.

How does Paul invade the kingdom of darkness? He follows Christ as he relies on God's strength, stands up, and walks straight into the dark world as an ambassador of light. How do you fight spiritual warfare? You rely, you stand, you walk into the dark world. It was prophesied that Christ would do it. He did it. We see how Paul did it. And he calls us to imitate him, just as he imitates Christ (1 Corinthians 11:1).

PRAYER—A VITAL PART OF OUR BATTLE

Jesus also models for us the importance of prayer in the midst of our battle with evil. Prayer is how we express our living dependence on God. It's how we rely on God's power for the help we need. When Satan attempted to gain moral authority over Jesus, seeking to shape Jesus's choices, Jesus fought in the Ephesians 6 way. He spent forty days with the Word of God and prayer in his heart and on his lips. It was intensive prayer and fasting. Of course. This is the invading Lord of Isaiah and Psalms, doing the very things Paul told us to do in putting on Christ. Jesus also knew that we needed his prayers. And so he prayed for us when he was on earth (John 17; Luke 22:32). And he is interceding for us now in heaven (Romans 8:34; Hebrews 7:25).

Because prayer is a vital part of how we fight against the powers of darkness, Paul ends his discussion of spiritual warfare in Ephesians in prayer. Leaving the weaponry metaphor behind, but continuing his warfare, Paul prays for others. His intercessions so seamlessly weave into all he says that it's hard to tell where his prayers end and his teaching picks up. His prayers are wondrously normal. These "warfare prayers" do not speak of or to Satan, but instead address our deepest need for Christ's presence and help. Paul's core intercession is very simple: "May God strengthen you to know him." No binding and loosing, no authoritative pronouncements and proclamations, no naming and claiming. He tells us to keep on "praying at all times in the Spirit, with all prayer and supplication" and to pray for "all the saints" (v. 18), and then goes on to ask for prayer for himself (v. 19).

As counselors, it's tempting for us to trust our theories of motivation and causality, and our knowledge of how people tend to react to certain struggles. It's easy to feel so confident in what we know that we don't depend on our good Shepherd for wisdom, help, and the power to change. But if you realize that there are forces at work bigger than you, it makes you really pray and really mean it.

You know that Jesus holds out life and mercy to people who don't want to know him: to the weak and ungodly, to sinners and enemies (Romans 5:6–10). He alone can set them free from deception. In part because of the devil, you are quickened to pray for—and with—those you counsel. In part because of the devil, you are quickened to lead them into the reality of the Savior of the world. Without him, they walk alone, relying on illusions in the face of deadly danger.

I've often been surprised that after I've prayed for someone who doesn't seem to be interested in God or able to hear the truth of the gospel, they come back and say, "That thing you said changed my life." Usually I can't remember saying anything like what they remember. Often it doesn't even sound like something I would have said! But something happened when the Holy Spirit took my pitiful prayers and turned them into groaning too deep for words (Romans 8:26–27). Those groanings landed in someone's life in a way that went beyond what I could do as a counselor. The reality of spiritual warfare teaches the counselor and the counselee about our constant need for dependence on the good Shepherd. We express that dependence as we pray at all times, for all the saints, and most especially for those that the Lord has entrusted to us to guide and help.

Here are some ideas on how to pray at all times for every saint:

- Pray for your friends and family. The people you are most connected to need the Lord to directly impart his strength for them to be able to walk in faith and love. What part of the armor of Christ do each of them need the most today? Pray that the Spirit would clothe them with Christ. Pray that their eyes would be open to their need for Christ.

- Pray for those you counsel. Pray that they would be drawn to a living dependence on Christ. That the strength and love of Christ would flow into their lives and flow toward others. Pray for their faith—that they would have ears to hear and eyes to see the love of God for them in Christ.

- Take the truth that has most struck you as you've been reading and pray for the Spirit to make this truth alive in your life. Now pray that it would also be alive in your pastor's life. Leadership is a very hard calling, and your leaders need much grace. If you are a pastor, pray for other pastors and leaders that you know.

- Pray for fellow Christians who either ignore spiritual warfare or exaggerate it. It is so important to get this right. We as God's children need to live in the real world—neither half asleep nor in a fantasy world.
- Ask others to pray for you. Paul knew he needed God to give him the words to say and the boldness to say it. What do you specifically need that only the Lord can give? Isn't it marvelous that the author of the New Testament's most exalted letter can include this request, *Make supplication for all the saints, and also for me?*!

If you are a Christian who counsels, how could you not fight spiritual warfare with and for the people you counsel? They need your help to stand up to the triad of world, flesh, and devil. In the next chapters we will explore what that looks like through different stories of spiritual warfare. The case studies illustrate how spiritual warfare is both mundane and profound. Spiritual warfare is a normal part of ministry to daily life struggles, because powerful forces are at work in what happens every day. From minor illnesses and interpersonal conflict, all the way to even the most bizarre phenomena—it all can be understood in the light of Ephesians 6, and we can learn to offer truth and bring gospel peace as Jesus himself did when facing evil of all kinds.

Chapter 5

FIGHTING THE NORMAL BATTLES: ANGER, FEAR, ESCAPISM

Most of the issues that bring people into counseling can be sorted into three general categories: anger, fear, and escapism. These are the normal battles that all of us face every day. As a counselor, you will hear people talk about these things in all different kinds of ways. Anger, at its extreme, might be expressed as explosive hostility or extreme bitterness, but it also encompasses everyday complaining and grumbling about traffic, coworkers, family, the weather, etc. Fear can be full-blown paranoia and paralyzing panic attacks, or it can be anxiety and worry about the smallest of things. Escapism can manifest as alcoholism and drug addiction, or a propensity to overeat and watch too much TV.

Understanding how spiritual warfare intersects with these common, everyday problems starts with remembering that the whole world is in the power of the Evil One (1 John 5:19). What is the Evil One like? He is a God-mimic. He is always seeking to mimic God and he wants us to imitate him and be God-mimics too. In all of these issues—anger, fear, and escapism—we have a choice. We can play God and thus imitate Satan, or we can go to God and cry to him for the help we need.

How does this play out when we are angry? If we are mimicking God instead of going to God, we become, like Satan, a false judge and an accuser (Revelation 12:10). James unpacks this dynamic in his letter (James 4:1–12). When we take on God's role as judge, we play the accuser. We become self-righteous, condemning, malicious, unfair. We actually end up lying to others, saying things like, "You always do this." "You never do that." We are defensive; we blame others; we are demanding, aggressive, merciless.

What about fear? Here we see Satan mimicking God as a false prophet. My colleague Ed Welch describes anxiety as a voice that tells us lies about ourselves, our God, our world, and about our future. What do people hear in their mind when they are anxious? "You have ruined everything." "If people really knew me, they would reject me." "God doesn't love me." "How could I ever be forgiven?" "You will never change." Everyone has their own list of lies about themselves and their future that they are tempted to believe. These are not the words God speaks in Scripture to his beloved children. These are words from the Evil One who has been a liar from the beginning. He lies to us about ourselves and our prospects in life. He is a false prophet.

What about escapism and addiction? The common theme that runs through addiction, escapism, and the wrong kind of pleasure-seeking is that we are taking refuge in a false savior. We are looking for something besides God to make us happy, to make us feel good, to help us deal with the unpleasant realities of our lives. Satan mimics God and presents himself as a false savior. He is continually proposing self-salvation schemes to people that are designed to keep them from the real Savior. His very first foray into human relationships was in the garden. He tempted Adam and Eve with the thought that they could save themselves and could be like God.

In these everyday issues, we can see how Satan, as the God-mimic, plays the judge, the prophet, and the savior. And we live in a world that agrees with every one of Satan's lies. But we are involved as well. Our hearts are always active. We choose to act like Satan as the judge and accuser. We listen to his false prophecies about ourselves and our future and forget to turn to the living God for the truth. We believe that we can find a different way to salvation than through Jesus Christ and pursue the carrot of self-salvation that Satan holds out. James says that ultimately we can't blame anyone but ourselves when we fall into temptation and sin (James 1:13–15). So when we struggle with anger, fear, and escapism we see all of our enemies at work. The world, the flesh, and the devil are all involved. This is a daunting trio. But our hope is embedded in what we have learned in Ephesians.

In Ephesians 6, Paul describes the Christian life in simple terms. If we strip the metaphor out, he is telling us about the seven basic elements of what it means to be strong in the Lord and in his might. What will make you and those you counsel able to stand against the world, the flesh, and the devil? Truth, righteousness, the gospel of peace, faith, salvation, the Word of God, and prayer. These are the everyday, normal stuff of the Christian life. They are what you, me, and your counselees need every day to stand against the world, the flesh, and the devil. It is what we have been given in Christ to live in the strength of Christ. It is what we have to offer to our counselees right in the middle of their everyday struggles with anger, fear, and escapism. There is hope for them and for you because Christ is our strength and he has provided specific ways for us to live in his strength.

COUNSELING AN ANGRY PERSON

Most of the angry people who come to you for counsel will be in the middle of a conflict. In our culture, anger and bitterness are often psychologized—as if the problem only exists in you. But it exists between people. Conflict is by definition interpersonal. It is not just a psychological problem; it is a relational problem between you and God, and between you and other people.

Satan works in that corporate, relational dimension. Our bitterness and anger give Satan the foothold that Paul warns the Ephesians about (Ephesians 4:26–27). Counseling with that in view means setting a vision for what is at stake. As you seek to reorient counselees, remind them that we have been given union with God in Christ. We are being remade in his image. In Christ's image our faith always expresses itself in love and forgiveness. We are living on a bigger stage. How we live by faith, and how we forgive, are all part of how the kingdom of God is coming to this world.

But just knowing those truths is not enough. When we are in the grip of anger and bitterness, James says that there is a demonic aspect to us (James 3:13–18). We resemble the liar and murderer in how we exalt ourselves and judge and damn others. But God gives more grace. We can resist the devil by humbling ourselves, and he will have to flee (James 4:6–10). We can only do this out of total dependence on the good Shepherd. Only he can help us to forgive and bless instead of accuse and curse. Helping someone understand and move forward means encouraging a living dependence on our living Savior, which is the #1 most important goal in any of our counseling.

COUNSELING A FEARFUL PERSON

What about someone who comes to you with crippling fear and anxiety? Where do the false predictions of the future come from? They come from the author of lies, the intimidator, and the accuser. Those lies that cause us so much fear, anxiety, and distress come from the one who has been lying from the beginning.

Anxiety, like anger, is often seen as a purely psychological, emotional problem. But anxiety also hinders us from caring about other people and reaching out of our own world toward others. Because we are afraid, the lies we believe isolate us from others. We are in a spiritual war in that very action, because withdrawal is loveless and faithless.

How do you talk to someone gripped by fear? You speak truth to them. The central promise of the Bible to fearful people is that "I am with you." Do not fear is a command that doesn't come with a warning (like the Ten Commandments); it comes with a promise of God's help and presence.[1] This is a gift that we can ask for. We don't have to listen to the lies of the Evil One. We can identify those lies and turn to God for help in our time of need. We can learn to hear the voice of the good Shepherd and go in and out with him (John 10:4). Once again we are back to the #1 goal—growing in a living dependency on our good Shepherd.

---

1. See, for example, Deuteronomy 31:6–8; Jeremiah 1:8; Matthew 14:27; Philippians 4:4–7.

COUNSELING THE ADDICT

How do we understand and help those struggling with addiction and pleasure-seeking? Often people think that demon deliverance is called for once a certain line has been crossed and "normal" sins (like too much shopping, eating, and playing video games) have progressed into bondage (like opioid addiction). But that view finds no support in the Bible. When Jesus defined Paul's ministry as turning people "from the power of Satan to God," he called him to proclaim the forgiveness of sins, repentance, and a new life that reflects a changed heart (Acts 26:18, 20). The power of Satan over someone's life always yields to repentance and faith in Christ.

How does anyone come to see? We see when the gospel is unveiled by the God whose power created the world and raised Jesus. If anyone awakens, it is because God shines the light of Christ Jesus into hearts (2 Corinthians 4:6). Sinners are blinded by the devil, and they culpably choose blindness. Everyone is a slave, but no one is a puppet. God enlightens; people turn and believe.

The Bible's most forceful portrayal of moral bondage occurs in 2 Timothy 2:25–26. Paul piles up words for slavery to Satan: morally ignorant, out of their minds, trapped by the devil, captured alive by him, obeying the devil's will. In the context, Paul describes how to do ministry to such people. Their slavery is more than matched by their deliverance: repentance leading to knowledge of the truth, coming to their senses, escaping the devil's trap, and being freed from captivity, so they no longer serve his will. What changes such people? "God may perhaps grant them repentance" (v. 25). There is no possibility of self-liberation, but there is no bondage too difficult. Nothing we can do can impart life or cast off chains. But we play a significant role. Given the magnitude of the problem, our part in the solution sounds astonishingly modest.

So flee youthful passions and pursue righteousness, faith, love, and peace, along with those who call on the Lord from a pure heart. Have nothing to do with foolish, ignorant controversies; you know that they breed quarrels. And the Lord's servant must not be quarrelsome but kind to everyone, able to teach, patiently enduring evil, correcting his opponents with gentleness. (2 Timothy 2:22–25)

Ministry to enslaved people begins with fleeing our own slavish propensities, bringing us into the community of those who call on the Lord and pursue Christ's character (note the parallels to the Ephesians' weaponry). We learn to do Christ's work of deliverance in Christ's way: breathing forth the fragrance of kindness, speaking relevant truth, being patient when others wrong us, correcting gently, relying on the Lord. Jesus can and does set slaves free, using us.

RESTORE CHOICE

One of the most elemental aspects of biblical counseling is the truth that people are always making a choice. They are always turning one way or the other. When you are angry, when you are anxious, when you want to escape, where do you choose to turn? Jeremiah describes a person who is turning away from God: "cursed is the man who trusts in man and makes flesh his strength, whose heart turns away from the Lord" (17:5). We might call this anti-repentance, since it is the opposite of true repentance, which is characterized by turning toward God. Jeremiah is describing someone who is turning away from the fountain of living water and is becoming like a dried-up bush that lives in the desert. That accurately describes those who are caught in anger, anxiety, and escapism.

One of the goals of pastoral counseling is to restore to people the awareness of choice in situations where they don't feel like they are choosing. Usually when you feel stuck in anger, anxiety, or escapist behavior, you don't think you can choose to desire, feel, think, and act differently. But for those in Christ, they have the power of Christ. They have Christ's strength, truth, and righteousness. They have the Word of Christ and the power of prayer.

How do you then help others understand that they can choose to turn to God? One of the simplest, and most effective homework assignments is a three-by-five card that has two choices—one written on each side. One choice is the anti-repentance and the other is the truth of God's Word applied to their particular struggle. One side would be the voice of the world, the flesh, and the devil that says, "You need to do this for reasons x, y, and z." The other side of the card would give words to what repentance and crying out to God would look like in the midst of the struggle that they are in. How will they turn to God in the midst of accusing others? What voice will they listen to when they hear the voice of the accuser? How will they choose when tempted to find salvation in someone or something that is not Christ? As you think through these questions together, you can help those you counsel come up with biblical, powerful, and concrete ways to turn toward Christ and rely on him in the midst of their everyday struggles. Because of Christ, they can choose Christ. Because of the Spirit, they can keep in step with the Spirit.

Turning to Christ is to win spiritual warfare.

Chapter 6

THE BATTLE WITH THE SHADOW OF DEATH

In 2003, our sixteen-year-old daughter was diagnosed with a rare, painful, and progressive illness. Its effects were potentially disfiguring, disabling, even deadly. The cause was a mystery. It had no cure. Some symptoms could be treated or would spontaneously abate. But one never knew when the next episode might strike, with ever-worsening symptoms. Doctors did say that in 30 percent of cases, for unknown reasons, the illness disappeared as mysteriously as it had appeared. If there was no recurrence and decline over the next three years, they would consider her cured. These were the particular circumstances in which our family needed to take up the shield of faith.

Facing a dire diagnosis, there are many ways to lose the spiritual battle, reverting to the darkness of flesh, world, and devil. Will we go blind to God, becoming absorbed in the immediate threat? Will we worry, feeling an undercurrent of anxiety or even stark fear? Will we obsess about medical intervention? Will we go into denial? Will we numb our apprehensions by escaping into work, TV, or drink? Will we get irritable with each other, exacerbating the tension by bickering? Will we become stoic, short-circuiting honest human need with a quick "God is in control" that is more Islamic than psalmic? Will we pray repetitively, even superstitiously? There are many ways to revert to the darkened understanding that expresses alienation from the life of God (Ephesians 4:17–18). The flaming darts of the Evil One aim to recapture us for the godless darkness.

We could revert, or we could face our troubles the way Ephesians and Psalms face trouble. In this situation, Psalm 28 gathered up our experience and took us in hand. It is one of many psalms in which human need finds God's strength and shielding care. This psalm walked us through our battle with the world, flesh, and devil during a difficult time. It puts feet on Ephesians 6. It gave us words. The psalm unfolds in four phases that I will introduce with a summary sentence in the first person.

I cry for help: Psalm 28:1–2. These first few lines give voice to a sense of utter need and great vulnerability in the face of threat.

> I call to you, O Lord, my rock.
> Do not turn a deaf ear to me.
> If you remain silent,
> I will become like those who go down to the pit.
> Hear my cry for mercy as I cry to you for help,
> as I lift up my hands toward your most holy sanctuary.

This is no routine "say your prayers." It's not just an item added to your prayer list. It's not just a change in your self-talk, as if faith's sphere of operations happens inside your mind: "Just remember that God is in control. Just remember your identity in Christ." Faith's sphere of operations is in relating to another: "I need you, merciful God, our King. When you consider my need, remember who you are. Remember your promises of compassion. Help us." Need cries out to one able and willing to help. The act of turning in actual need to the Lord was an act of sanity and light.

Our family cried out to our Lord.

I name the evils I am facing: 28:3–5. In the next few lines, David grapples with the specific evils animating this plea for mercies. In his situation (replicated for Jesus a millennium later), he faced the enmity of godless men who did the evils that their hearts incubated. In our situation, other people were not attacking us. Rather, here are the four enemies that came into play for our family as we faced my daughter's illness.

- The Enemy worked to blind and confuse us, attempting to reassert mastery over us by deforming us back into his image. He operated within our temptations to anxiety, escapism, anger, and the rest. (Matthew 13:39; Luke 10:19; Ephesians 6:11–13)
- Our daughter's illness was a precursor of the Last Enemy, a shadow of death darkening the steps of a sixteen-year-old girl. (1 Corinthians 15:26)
- The inner enemy was revealed in the "passions of our flesh . . . the desires of the body and the mind" (Ephesians 2:2–3). Our own hearts manifest a sympathy for the devil. Would we insist on healing? Would we demand a comfortable life? Would we place our deepest hopes in doctors? Would we be gripped by fear? We would become obsessive, angry, escapist, or anxious if we were driven by the tyranny of the desires of body and mind.

- The world around us was a subtler human enemy. Ephesians 4:14 warns of the false messages blowing around us. Anyone facing illness simultaneously faces widely enculturated and well-institutionalized assumptions. The air we breathe insinuates an ideology and value system: good health, medical care, and medical cure are the *summum bonum* (rather than a *bonum*). Would we be misled, and never realize what was shaping our attitudes and choices?

We need to take up the shield of faith "in all circumstances." Psalm 28:3–5 flags human enemies. But the same pattern of faith applies when we face other grievous circumstances where we need God's strength and shield.

In our plea for mercy, we named the exact evils we were facing and spoke about them to the Lord.

I rejoice in my strength and shield (28:6–7). This psalm moves quickly across the emotional register, arriving at joyful peace far more quickly than we did. Scripture is giving us a template, not a timetable. David is showing us the direction in which to walk:

> The LORD is my strength and my shield.
> In him my heart trusts, and I am helped.
> My heart exults, and with my song I give thanks to him.

It is striking how the general exhortations of Ephesians 6:10–20 and 5:18–20 recapitulate these exact themes. Honest gratitude and joy are intrinsic to spiritual warfare. God's Spirit creates exultation and thankfulness throughout Ephesians, as in many psalms. Spiritual warfare is not grim or apprehensive, not paranoid or superstitious, not magical or talismanic. The Lord proved to be our strength and shield in the crisis. And, mercifully, our daughter's symptoms abated. Months passed, and then years. We did not forget the threat, though it became distant with time. We trusted, and we were helped.

That was not the end of this story. A bolt out of the blue hit exactly three years later. Our daughter was in Uganda for a semester abroad. The university doctor was instructing the students on the importance of the anti-malarial medicine they were taking. He mentioned in passing that this medicine could trigger the rare syndrome that she had faced. She was shaken by the memory and the possibility. She changed medicines. We trusted, and we were helped. She did fine.

What if our daughter's condition had degraded rather than improved? What if she was not fine now, but her body had become inflamed and broken with pain? That would be a hard road, bringing many temptations. But the path of life that Ephesians and the Psalms mark out for us would still be the path of life. We'd seek, find, and rejoice in the strength and shield that the Lord provides in all circumstances.

I intercede for others: Psalm 28:8–9. This psalm concludes the same way that Ephesians 6:18–20 concludes. David reaches beyond himself, and reaches out for others who need what he has been given.

> The LORD is the strength of his people.
> He is the saving refuge of his anointed.
> Oh, save your people and bless your heritage!
> Be their shepherd and carry them forever.

David professes faith in the Lord's strength for all his brothers and sisters. He intercedes for God's people. We need the strength, refuge, and the saving care of the Lord our shepherd. David is praying for us.

You face the same variety of enemies, temptations, and struggles that David did, that Jesus did, that my family did. We needed our Lord to strengthen and shield us. You need the same. I pray that this very story might be a gift that leads you to know more deeply the ways of our Christ through the wisdom of Psalm 28 and Ephesians.

Chapter 7

IN CONFLICT WITH THE OCCULT

It is often argued that people with a history of occult involvement need some sort of demon deliverance. This is invariably paired with firsthand experiences of how deeply people become enmeshed in darkness, how difficult it is to break free, how confused or vile they become, and the almost palpable aura of evil that such people emit. But in interpreting and responding to such experiences, would-be helpers often ignore the Bible's striking examples of those who traffic with the dark side. The pattern of ministry and description of the change process is strikingly uniform. It is consistently and vividly "normal." Deliverance from the sign of pursuing the occult never includes any sort of deliverance from inhabiting spirits.[1] We will consider three examples.

First, Manasseh did it all when it came to the "despicable practices of the nations" (2 Kings 21:2). His biography reads

---

1. Acts 16:16–18 is seemingly an exception to this comment. See footnote 3 on p. 65.

like an encyclopedia article on occult involvement: worshiping multiple idols; burning his sons in human sacrifice; using fortune-telling, omens, and sorcery; and consulting mediums and necromancers. Manasseh also murdered others besides his sons; he "filled Jerusalem with innocent blood" (2 Kings 24:4). It sounds like dry understatement when the list of his vile and violent transgressions concludes, "He did much evil in the sight of the LORD, provoking him to anger" (2 Kings 21:6).

So what happened to Manasseh? The prophets pointedly spoke the Lord's words to Manasseh (2 Kings 21:10; 2 Chronicles 33:18). He paid no attention. God brought painful consequences on him. He was captured with hooks, bound in chains, and led in exile. Then Manasseh changed. In the midst of his distress, he humbled himself before God, pleading for mercy. God was moved by his plea and mercifully restored him. Manasseh lived out his days as a man of faith (2 Chronicles 33:10–20).

Notice the pattern: (1) deep immersion in vile practices; (2) pointed ministry of the Word; (3) negative consequences for intransigence; (4) deeply repentant faith; (5) restoration and a fruitful life. The degree of spiritual perversity in his sin did not change either the mode of ministry or the dynamics of change. Later we will look at how Scripture portrays the casting out of demons. Here it is worth noting that when the problem is moral bondage to Satan, demon deliverance is never the practice.

Second, Philip was proclaiming Christ in Samaria, where a man named Simon practiced magic arts with great power (Acts 8:9–24). When Simon heard the gospel, he believed and was baptized. He saw signs and works of power done through Philip, including casting out unclean spirits and other healings (8:6–7, 13). He saw the Holy Spirit given through Peter's and John's hands, and he offered money to get that power for himself. Many Christians would immediately suspect a demonic stronghold at work in Simon's soul, "a bat in the cave" from his pre-conversion life. As a ministry approach, they would seek to cast it out.

If exorcism were the way to deal with the sins of the occult practitioner, it would seem that this is the time. Demon-deliverance healings are taking place right in the context. But Peter goes in a completely different direction. He speaks point-edly to Simon, holding the man responsible for both behavior and motives, calling him to repentance. Here are Peter's words (Acts 8:20–23, emphasis added):

> But Peter said to him, "May *your* silver perish with *you*, because *you thought you* could obtain the gift of God with money! *You* have neither part nor lot in this matter, for *your heart is not right* before God. *Repent*, therefore, *of this wickedness of yours*, and *pray* to the Lord that, if possible, *the intent of your heart* may be forgiven *you*. For I see that *you are in the gall of bitterness and in the bond of iniquity*."

This is the most extended personal reproof in the entire Bible. It is sinful to engage in occult practices and to covet. And these sins are dealt with by repentance, not exorcism.

Third, it is worth noting that when the good news of Jesus Christ broke out to the nations, most first-century Christian converts came from a background of idolatry, polytheism, occult practices, and demon worship. The exceptions to this rule are pointed out: monotheistic Jews and their Gentile followers, and a few rationalistic philosophers (Acts 17). But the major-ity worshiped the dark side. The New Testament epistles were written to them. That's where we learn how the church is to do ministry: speaking truth that is pointedly convicting and full of mercies, praying honestly and dependently, living what we say we believe, worshiping together, doing genuine good to meet human need, admitting and repenting of our failures, and so forth. The fact that a person came from an occult background did not change the game plan. In our contemporary Western world, overt idolaters, occult practitioners, and Satan worshipers stand out as unusual (but this is not true for most of the world still). Paul, Peter, James, and John developed a game plan for such people—the "normal" ministry methods. These methods are designed for such sins, as well as every other form of sin.

UNDERSTANDING EXORCISMS IN MATTHEW, MARK, LUKE, AND ACTS

In light of that, you might be wondering how to understand Jesus's exorcisms in the Gospels and the exorcisms that his followers were involved in that are recorded in Acts. The books of Matthew, Mark, Luke, and Acts proclaim numerous works of power whereby Jesus and the apostles perform healings by casting out evil spirits. This brings joy to those who had suffered and amazement to those who witness the display of merciful power. In various works of mercy, Jesus shows his divine power: he feeds the hungry, stills a storm, heals the sick, casts out demons, raises the dead, even procures tax money for Peter—all at a word of command or a touch of his hands.[2]

---

2. It is beyond the scope of this chapter to explore other questions about how Jesus's mercy ministry (and now ours) alleviates suffering. For example, Jesus's mode of doing good is by dramatic, performative words and actions. For us, the mode of doing good changes into dependent prayer and loving action. This has wide-ranging implications for how we approach healing of afflictions whatever their cause. For a discussion of the significance of the mode of doing ministry, see the Appendix, which includes an excerpt from *Power Encounters* by David Powlison (pp. 77–92 reprinted by permission).

The Bible never connects these deliverances to Satan's *moral lordship* and our battle with sin. They are part of mercy ministry to sufferers, not our fight against the triumvirate of dark masters. In the Gospels and Acts, supposed "demons" of sin (e.g., pride, anger, lust, addiction) are never identified, spoken to, bound, or cast out. Sins are not even mentioned as bringing on the afflictions and disabilities caused by demons.

All sufferings ultimately connect to the curse on sin, but the Gospels head in a different direction: mercy to sufferers is the constant theme (with warnings of curses for the unrepentant). In the Old Testament, Saul was punished for his sins by a tormenting evil spirit sent from God (1 Samuel 16:14–23). The evil spirit neither caused Saul's sins, nor held him in bondage. It inflicted pain because of Saul's sins. David's music (singing psalms?) drove off the spirit and alleviated the pain.

As with the man born blind, the point was not who had sinned but that the merciful works of God might be displayed in Jesus (John 9:3). It's a sign of the Messiah when good things happen in a world where suffering and anguish always seem to have the last say.

Demon deliverance in the Bible is a subset of the category of healing.[3] In the Bible some afflictions have a demonic cause; others have other causes. This is clear not only in individual incidents, but also in the summary of Jesus's works. For example:

---

3. The one exception occurs in Acts 16:16–18, where a slave girl had a spirit that enabled divination and fortune telling. Paul ignored her for many days. Finally, out of annoyance (!), he tells the spirit to get lost. The exception proves the rule. The girl is portrayed as a slave, both to human masters who exploit her and to the paranormal gifts of a dark spirit. As with every exorcism, the story never even hints at the girl's possible sins (pursuit of an occult power? Unbelief?). She had heard the word of Christ repeatedly, and there is no evidence that the message was met with faith.

And he went throughout all Galilee, teaching in their synagogues and proclaiming the gospel of the kingdom and healing every disease and every affliction among the people. So his fame spread throughout all Syria, and they brought him all the sick, those afflicted with various diseases and pains, those oppressed by demons, those having seizures, and paralytics, and he healed them. (Matthew 4:23–24; cf. Luke 7:21)

Demonization is an item on the list of sufferings to be cured. In the Bible's descriptions of demon deliverance, people afflicted by demons are blind or deaf, crippled or convulsive—or in the most extreme cases, driven to madness by unlocalized pain and torment (Mark 5:1–20; cf. 1 Samuel 16:14–23). Their sufferings have a demonic agency; Jesus heals them. Even in places where a demonic voice cries out through a person and speaks in recognition of Jesus (e.g., Mark 5:7–12; Luke 4:34), the Bible never makes the point that the person was sinfully participating. Every incident is simply portrayed as a merciful healing, demonstrating that Jesus is the Messiah and giving us reasons to believe.

No moral stigma is assigned to being painfully afflicted. In fact, the most plausible interpretation of Paul's thorn in the flesh, "a messenger of Satan to harass me" (2 Corinthians 12:7), is a demonically caused physical torment. Not only is Paul's physical tormentor not connected to any moral stigma or habitual sin, but also the painful weakness actually serves to guard Paul from the sin of conceit, keeping him dependent on God's mercy and power (2 Corinthians 12:7–9).

The temporary alleviation of the suffering of others played a particular role in Jesus's overall mission. Jesus's mercy ministry does sheer good, rolling back the curse. These healings, feedings, stilling of a storm, and resurrections are true goods—but they are temporary. They point to something better by far. Every person healed, fed, saved from drowning, or raised, later suffered and died in some other way. Jesus was on a mission to win the ultimate cosmic warfare. The Gospel of John never mentions a demonized sick person, but it proclaims the supreme "exorcism." When Jesus says, "Now will the ruler of this world be cast out" (John 12:31–33), he points to the cosmic exorcism of all that is wrong—sin, death, and Satan—overcome forever by the death, resurrection, and return of the Lamb of God. Even so, come Lord Jesus.

Chapter 8

THE BATTLE WITH ANIMISM

Christians often argue that people living in animistic contexts need some special sort of demon deliverance. Some believe that a history of occult practices and beliefs necessitates a kind of ministry that is completely different from Ephesians 6. This may initially seem plausible because the phenomena and symptoms are bizarre. But as we've seen, Scripture gives striking examples of occult practitioners being ministered to by normal, biblical spiritual warfare: for example, Manasseh (2 Kings 21; 2 Chronicles 33) and Simon (Acts 8). Here is a contemporary story that corroborates with what Scripture leads us to expect.

A European friend of mine went to rural West Africa in the 1980s as a long-term missionary. He taught in a theological college, did church planting, and pastoral ministry. When he arrived, the implicit rationalism of his Western worldview was blown away by the disturbing forces he encountered: animism, witchcraft, amulets, manifestations of bizarre voices and various other physical effects, trance states and hallucinations, a visceral sense of being in the presence of uncanny evil. He encountered these phenomena both in professing Christians and in non-Christians. He began to adopt the common demon-deliverance version of spiritual warfare, and experienced apparent success.

But as time went by, he increasingly doubted both the legitimacy and efficacy of what he was doing. For one thing, a deliverance event, however dramatic in the moment, proved to be no predictor of any good thing in a person's life over the long term. It did not result in blessing, or stability, or spiritual growth, or freedom from symptoms. In contrast, those who turned from their sins and came under Christ *did* live changed lives. Those whose lives became fruitful were people who did the normal things of faith. Normal did not mean rote, perfunctory, or mechanical. It meant embracing Scripture, honest confession and repentance, candid faith in prayer and worship, vital fellowship and accountability, and practical obedience—what this book has been about. But the people in whom normal things did not take root continued to live in sin, fear, and animistic chaos.

As my friend continued to reflect on Scripture and his experience, he concluded that the view and practice of demon deliverance was a failure and did not add up biblically. So what was going on with the darkly bizarre symptoms that he was encountering? The Evil One and his agents *were* intimately involved. But most of the varied phenomena—the sense of uncanny moral evil, the lies, fear, confusion, and hostility—point toward normal human experience in a world of suffering. As touched on in the discussion of Psalm 28, people suffer terribly under many things: the hardships of disease and poverty, hostility and injustice from others, anguish of conscience, the cruelty of the Slave Master, the imminent threat of death. It is always right to earnestly cry out to God, "Deliver us from evil. Be merciful, O Lord." But the animistic worldview provided the suggestion that the brokenness of life calls for a power encounter with an inhabiting spirit. My friend came to see the deeper human need and began to change his approach.

He started to dig carefully, to proceed more patiently, to do more pointed ministry of Word and prayer. He sought to find out what else was going on in the lives of people. He found dark secrets and relational problems—and the miseries of life that both tempt to sin and result from sin. He found secret adulteries. He found financial corruption. He found Christians who, in their anguish over a sick child or extreme poverty, began visiting witch doctors and wearing amulets. Most frequently, he found bitterness and hatred, relationships that had been broken and never reconciled. False accusations were also a common relational problem. In the context of suffering and unexpected death, the traditional culture looked for someone to blame. The finger of accusation often pointed to "witches" or "witch children" as the cause.[1]

In all these cases, bizarre manifestations appeared. The Liar, Accuser, and Murderer is at work in all this—but not in the way it was being interpreted. The animistic worldview they lived within was yet another lie—a "teaching" that comes from demons about demons, fueling superstition and fear (1 Timothy 4:1). My friend was uncovering complex spiritual and moral problems, but there was no need to sort out where "flesh" ends and "world" begins, where "world" ends and "devil" begins. The forces of evil work in concert. We don't need to determine where the devil's role in moral blinding and in inflicting destruction begin and end. We can't see through the fog of war. But Christ's truth and power address all dimensions

---

1. Even secular studies of witchcraft observe that relationship breakdowns lie behind the bizarre phenomena, and that the problem is solved by confession and forgiveness.

simultaneously. We intercede with our Lord to comprehensively deliver us from evil.

My friend normalized the abnormal and humanized the bizarre, seeking to get behind confusing appearances, seeking to minister. He dealt with bizarre evil the way the Bible tells us to deal with evil of any sort: clear scriptural truth; bold, faith-expressing prayers that plead the mercies and power of Christ; heartfelt worship; meaningful fellowship. People brought their sins, fears, and confusion to the light. They found Christ's mercy and aid and acted in newness of life. The bizarre symptoms disappeared. Biblical reality increasingly supplanted their false worldview.

My friend had come to mission work with a Christian faith tilted toward Western rationalism. The initial shock of cross-cultural experience had tilted his faith toward the traditional animistic worldview. Further ministry experience and biblical reflection increasingly shaped a humble, bold, truth-speaking, prayerful, loving approach to people.

True spiritual warfare normalizes the abnormal, helps people live in Christ's reality, not the haunted universe of animism. He was waging true spiritual warfare against the powers that enslave people in the confusion of sin and fear.

Chapter 9

SPIRITUAL WARFARE FOCUSES
ON THE PERSON

All people need ministry of the Word and prayer. Ministry is always called for, alongside other appropriate care, even when physiological factors are certain or highly likely to be involved (e.g., the dementias of aging, some depressions, brain injuries, schizophrenia, opioid addiction). We offer loving, candid, prayerful ministry to people who suffer other physical ailments—cancer, diabetes, post-surgical pain. All the more we can reach out to people whose problems have destructive mental, emotional, and relational effects. There is always a person inside every physical problem. A true understanding of spiritual warfare meets the person at the point of deepest need for strength and wisdom, whatever may be going on physically.

This story is about a colleague and friend. He is a wise counselor, with a marked ability to keep his bearings amid bizarre, complicated problems. He loves very troubled people. One Sunday after church, he heard a commotion in the fellowship hall, and went to find out what was going on. A slender, twenty-something woman was out of control, writhing on the floor, biting people, switching between several different personalities and voices, screaming hysterically, growling blasphemies in a deep animalistic voice, trying to escape. A group of people had gathered close around her. Some were attempting to physically restrain her, but she exhibited herculean strength, and they couldn't control her writhing. Others were praying loudly and authoritatively over her, attempting to cast out demons. One man in particular, a veteran of "warfare ministry," was taking charge in a confident, domineering manner. He interpreted her strength, her growling, blasphemous voice, and multiple personalities to mean that demons had taken over and were using her as their mouthpiece. He interpreted her cowering as "the demons are afraid" because he was binding them and commanding them to depart.

My friend is a respected elder and was able to get the group to back off. He sat down on the floor about eight feet away from the woman and talked quietly and reassuringly with her. She began to calm down enough to respond. She was exhausted by the intensity of what had happened but was able to speak rationally and start to unpack the incident. That first conversation was the start of a fruitful pastoral friendship. It led to hours of conversation between them over the weeks that followed. She was an extremely fearful person who projected a sense of overwhelming fragility and vulnerability. It came out that she had never been able to come to terms with being sexually abused as a young teen (something that many exorcism ministries interpret as opening a door to demon inhabitants). She'd been unable to tell anyone, even her parents. A sense of pain, horror, and threat never left her. She couldn't shake vivid memories of horrible things that the rapist said to her. She could find no words for her experience of unspeakable evil—only helpless agony. In daily life, she often felt on the verge of shattering into a thousand tiny pieces. When other people got too close, violating her physical or psychological space, she would violently react, flipping into multiple personality episodes. She was filled with an all-consuming sense of shame and personal dirtiness, afraid of exposure before the eyes of others. Her universe was fear-colored. Whenever the fear level started to rise inside, she had no resources, no idea of how to turn to Christ for help. She had no refuge and strength, no very present help in her very real troubles.

Why had she flipped out that morning after church? Why did she manifest multiple personalities? Why did she act and sound like an animal? It is a puzzle about which we do well to remain agnostic. Giving her a descriptive label like Multiple Personality Disorder or Dissociative Identity Disorder explains little, if anything. Naming her problems as demonic inhabitants is unhelpful speculation. People in the Bible whose physical sufferings were demonically induced didn't do and say the kinds of things she did and said. Labels and speculations also distract us from caring well for a troubled young woman, and learning what was going on inside her, and offering her real help.

Later, she was able to talk about what had happened that morning. She had felt distressed and began to fall apart. When people began crowding her, loudly and authoritatively invading her physical and psychological space, it had utterly terrified her. Hearing her problems named as demons had utterly terrified her. Her own hysterical reactions had utterly terrified her. But my friend's firm and unassuming human kindness and simple good sense slowly reassured her. He was able to draw her out. As he got to know her better, could he explain every kink and wrinkle in this young woman's life? No. Could he explain the unspeakable evil of what had happened to her? No. But where we find the reign of fear, lies, pain, violence, oppression, shame, stifling darkness, confusion—we know that these are characteristics of Satan's kingdom, not Christ's. My friend worked with what the Bible teaches us to know, normalizing the abnormal and humanizing the bizarre.

What helped this young woman? Initially he prayed silently for her (God hears and answers honest intercession, not according to the volume level). He talked gently with her (not bypassing her by loudly challenging supposed demonic agencies). Eventually he prayed clearly with her and for her (not praying loudly against supposed demons). Over time he lived, modeled, and communicated how Christ meets a very fearful young woman (not how the animistic view feeds fears). His prayers and counsel gathered up her sufferings and fears within the promises of our Lord's mercies and shielding strength. They talked about listening to God's voice. They exposed the false authority of the rapist's contrary voice. He was a liar, and the murderer of a girl's innocence, in the image of the Liar and Murderer. How might she put her hopes in Christ, rather than in the vain hope that her past would somehow go away? They talked about small obediences—what Ephesians 4:29 words might look like as she entered into conversations with people at church and the small practicalities of building genuine, mutual friendships. They talked about being known fully by God and loved. My friend's conversations embodied the things he spoke about. They became able to talk about her fears of people with depth and directness. Her world became organized. As inner panic lost its dominion, outer hysteria was no longer her only option. She learned to name evil—the real evils of sin and being sinned-against, the real devil who lies and kills, not the spooks of the animistic worldview—and to call on the name of the Lord. As she began to connect Christ's safe and strengthening truth to her honest experience, she began to learn faith. And she began to learn love.

In other words, my friend practiced spiritual warfare with her, seeking to set her free from the voices of world, flesh, and devil. He taught her how to fight, how to find strength in the God of strength, and shelter in the God who shields. She was learning to pray meaningfully. She was learning to trust, learning to stand against the world of fear. She was learning to love, learning to stand against the world of hate. She was learning to live within the body of Christ, the light of the world. In a world that often feels precarious, because it is precarious, she was learning to stand up to darkness.

Did this young woman's problems all go away? Of course not. She was coming out of a deep pit, and that's almost always a long process. But she subsequently spoke of that time after church as a true turning point. The bizarre experience forced her to consider crucial spiritual realities with more urgency: Who is in control? Who is her rock and fortress? Who does she trust? Trusting herself was no longer a viable option.

True spiritual warfare looks beyond the problems and sees the person.

Chapter 10

THE LAST BATTLE

As a counselor, you will have many opportunities to walk with people as they face death. You will also certainly face this battle yourself. This is a battle we will all face one day. Despite advances in medical care, the death rate remains steady. We will all die. My pastor has a line that I've always loved. He says, "In the end, doctors lose one hundred percent of their patients, but some of my patients live forever!"

What does this battle look like? And how do we encourage those we speak with to live in hope in the face of a serious diagnosis and their own death? We rightly think of Satan as a tempter, liar, and slave master, but he is ultimately bent on murder. In the Garden of Eden, Satan set out to murder Adam and Eve. His lies and schemes are always in service of his overall goal to kill and destroy. When Adam and Eve believed his lie—"you will not surely die"—and ate the fruit, death entered our world. Adam and Eve did die and ever since we too have been, as Hebrews says, subject to a lifelong slavery because of our fear of death (Hebrews 2:15).

Hebrews is not only describing the subjective feelings of fear, anxiety, and trepidation in the face of death, but also the objective reality that for all of us, whether we consciously acknowledge it or not, death will extinguish our lives. Without Christ, death gets the last say. So even if someone is cynical, cocky, or indifferent about death, they are still enslaved. They will have to bow before death one day.

How amazing then is the good news that Christ is alive! Here is how Hebrews explains how Jesus freed us from our slavery to death.

> Since therefore the children share in flesh and blood, he himself likewise partook of the same things, that through death he might destroy the one who has the power of death, that is, the devil, and deliver all those who through fear of death were subject to lifelong slavery. (Hebrews 2:14–15)

Jesus became flesh and blood, so that he could fully enter into our life and fully enter into our death. But he didn't die for his own sins. He had none. As the perfect man, he could give his life for his people. When the Innocent One gave himself for the sins of the world, the power of death was broken. As the lion Aslan explains to Lucy and Susan in *The Lion, the Witch, and the Wardrobe,* "when a willing victim who had committed no treachery was killed in a traitor's stead, the Table would crack and Death itself would start working backwards."[1] Jesus's life,

---

1. C. S. Lewis, *The Lion, the Witch, and the Wardrobe* (New York: Macmillan Publishing Co., 1970), 160.

death, and resurrection destroyed the one who has the power of death—the devil—and set free those who look to Jesus in faith.

When we face death, we have the same choice before us as we have in every area of life: Who will be our shepherd? Psalm 49 is about the foolish pride of humans and one line captures how life turns out for those who don't listen to their good Shepherd, "death shall be their shepherd" (v. 14). Their lives, as Psalm 1 points out, will turn to chaff, and everything they have done will turn to dust and fly away.

As a counselor, you have the privilege and opportunity to share with others how knowing Jesus makes all of the difference in this battle. Those who trust in him have a good Shepherd. With Christ, "the Lord is my shepherd," and all things are gained. We gain life now and forever as we walk with our good Shepherd through the valley of the shadow of death into the house of the Lord forever (Psalm 23). These are the realities that should frame the way we envision and do battle when we encounter the shadows of death and death itself. Yes, we are facing our enemies—the world, the flesh, and the devil. But our ultimate victory is guaranteed. The greatest good is not the physical healing of ourselves and those we love. The greatest gift is faith in Jesus—the One who defeated death for us and who will guide us safely home at just the right time. He is the one who provides the armor so that we can stand against the Evil One. And we do desperately need Christ's armor for this battle. It is a battle for faith, hope, and love in the middle of one of the hardest circumstances.

Six months ago, I was diagnosed with stage four pancreatic cancer. As I write, I am facing the real possibility of my own death. By God's grace I have been able to continue working, yet much of my work is bittersweet. I am handing off responsibilities and jobs to others. I am involved in making plans for the future that I am not likely to be a part of here on earth. Our family continues to grow with grandchildren. I wonder if I will be here to meet my next grandchild. Those I love are also in the midst of this battle with me—my wife, children, grandchildren, extended family, friends, friends at work. We are all confronted with the evil of death and illness. In the midst of this battle, the weapons Christ gives sustain and equip us to battle against the last enemy—death itself.

In this battle, grief is a reality. But like any human experience, the important thing is what you do with it. Where does the grief go? Where do you go? I have been with people who were facing their death and they were immobilized, almost frozen in the face of their grief. They couldn't talk about it and no one else could talk to them. Their grief reverberated through their life and become magnified until it filled their whole existence.

Grief is not wrong. It can be an honest expression of sorrow over the brokenness of this world. It can include a turning toward God for help and believing that our tears are counted and saved by the good Shepherd who hears and sees our suffering (Psalm 56:8). It is part of being made in the image of God to grieve hard things. When Jesus was facing the cross, he was grieving. He said, "Let this cup pass from me" as he cried and sweated blood (Matthew 26:39).

On the cross, Jesus quoted two psalms of great affliction, grief, and heartbreak. He cried out, "My God, my God why have you forsaken me?" (Psalm 22:1) and, as he breathed his last, "Into your hands I commit my spirit" (Psalm 31:5). Yet the direction his grief went was not hopelessness and despair. As a man who trusted God fully in the valley of death, hope and joy reverberates from his grief. Hebrews says that he went to the cross for "the joy set before him" (Hebrews 12:2). Jesus knew God's Word and he trusted in his heavenly Father. So, just as he withstood Satan's temptations in the wilderness, he was also able to stand against Satan's temptation to despair. On the cross he is utterly powerless. He is utterly dependent. He can't raise himself. He must depend on his Father. He's dependent on the Spirit of Life to rescue him from death. So he casts himself into God's care—and he died in faith. His death now opens the way for us to also face death by committing our spirits into our heavenly Father's hands.

Today I am called to fight this final battle with Jesus as my armor and his Spirit as my strength. I am experiencing the same kinds of temptations we faced when our daughter was ill. The world tells us that medicine is our only hope. We don't want to get fixated on finding a cure. We want to be wise. So we pray. We armor ourselves with the truth that the Lord is near and will be our good Shepherd. We take up the sword of the Spirit and remember Jesus's words that "sufficient for the day is its own trouble" and ask for help one day at a time (Matthew 6:34).

The temptation to slide off into various escapes is also present—television, sports, food. My escapism takes an unusual turn: I am burying my nose in a long biography of Joseph Stalin. Nothing really wrong with reading! But the temptation to not engage is present. Yet I hear the voice of my good Shepherd. I remember Jesus on the cross, facing death, yet still fully engaged with life—caring for his mother, speaking words of life to the thief next to him—and I can stay engaged too. I can pray with and for my wife Nan, my family, my friends, those I work with. I can trust their care to the great Shepherd of the sheep.

The temptation to listen to the lies of Satan is certainly still present. I have devoted my life to helping people know how central and relevant Christ and his Word is to the real things they struggle with personally, interpersonally, and situationally. But I also know how many other voices are clamoring for people's attention. Voices that shout, "We can explain your anxiety," "We can solve your depression," and "We can give you three tips that will improve your communication." I know that it's easy to listen to the voices of the world, the flesh, and the devil. I know that our grasp of truth can be fragile. I am concerned that fidelity to the Scripture will be embodied, carried forward, and that we will step out and tackle the next set of challenges in a way that's faithful to Jesus. When I worry, I turn to Christ. I gird myself with the belt of truth from the sword of the Spirit because it is Jesus who builds his church and the gates of hell cannot stand against it (Matthew 16:18).

As I reflect on this last battle, I can see that the Lord has been preparing me for this battle through my whole life. My conversion to Christ was cued by experiencing the death of two people. One was a young man who was killed in a car accident. The other was my grandfather. Both deaths were like a pebble in my shoe. They nagged at me. How could the life of a young person be snuffed out in a second? How could you get to the end of a long life and be in a kind of existential despair? I didn't have an answer. I began to see just a glimpse of how I was enslaved by the inevitability of my own death.

In the midst of my confusion, unbelief, and fear of death, God used Ezekiel 36:25–27 to bring me to faith. It was my first encounter with the belt of truth that Jesus gives his people. It was my first encounter with the sword of the Spirit that exposes and heals. At that moment, I knew the truth of what Paul wrote to the Corinthians, "For God, who said, 'Let light shine out of darkness,' has shone in our hearts to give the light of the knowledge of the glory of God in the face of Jesus Christ" (2 Corinthians 4:6). It was God who shone his light into my heart and awakened me from the slumber of sin and death.

Now more than four decades later, I am staring death in the face. Instead of my faith failing, the promise of a new heart holds true. God is still shining into the darkness of my heart to give me the knowledge of the glory of God in the face of Christ. The reality of death has made the truth of God's Word come alive to me. I am now living out the end of 2 Corinthians 4:

> So we do not lose heart. Though our outer self is wasting away, our inner self is being renewed day by day. For this light momentary affliction is preparing for us an eternal weight of glory beyond all comparison, as we look not to the things that are seen but to the things that are unseen. For the things that are seen are transient, but the things that are unseen are eternal. (vv. 16–18)

At times I am tempted to lose heart. But my good Shepherd is leading me toward life, not death. One of my favorite hymns is "My Song Is Love Unknown" written by Samuel Crossman in the seventeenth century. It begins, "Love to the loveless shown that they might lovely be." And then goes on, "Oh my friend, my friend indeed, who at my need his life did spend." Since the first day the Lord invaded my heart with his mercy and grace, I have never lost that sense of the friendship of Jesus, that he showed love to the loveless to make them lovely, that he befriended the friendless, that he befriended the unfriendly that were self-absorbed and all about themselves. That is the gospel of peace. My feet are fitted for this battle with my final enemy. So I do not lose heart. As Nan and I pray together, we do not lose heart. And even if I did or she did, God's mercy and grace would remain unchanging. We can always turn and ask for help in our time of need. He is always near.

This is what the whole Bible is about. It's about life and death; it's about what is going to happen to you when you die; it's about right and wrong, true and false, hope and despair, obedience and recklessness, faith and idolatry. This is the drama that we and those we minister to are living in. And the miracle is that we are given a new heart, a heart of flesh, and a new spirit so that we can and will live forever. What a privilege it has been for me to serve my faithful Savior these many years. What a privilege it has been to walk with others in need. And what a joy it will be to see him face to face.

Lord, you are the strength of your people. Save your people. Bless your heritage. Be their shepherd and carry them. Thank you that those who look to you in faith will be forever safe and sound.

On June 7, 2019, David died as he lived—depending on Jesus.

Appendix

JESUS'S MODE OF MINISTRY AND OURS

The ekballistic mode (EMM)[1] of redressing suffering does not stand alone among Jesus's mighty works of compassion and self-revelation. He performed many dramatic signs of power: he cast out demons, healed the sick, raised the dead and was raised himself, walked on the water, multiplied loaves and fish, and so forth. There are some obvious discontinuities between what Jesus did and what we are to do; there are also continuities. Scripture teaches us to discern the difference.

In this appendix we will look at eleven examples of Jesus's works that we are called to do in a fashion different from our master. Notice three things about each example. First, Jesus

---

1. The term "ekballistic mode of ministry" (EMM) describes the demon-deliverance movement. I first used this term in the book *Power Encounters: Reclaiming Spiritual Warfare*. Ekballistic comes from the Greek word *ekballo* which means to "cast out." For more background on this term, see *Power Encounters*, p. 28, now available online at newgrowthpress.com.

addresses genuine human needs that continue today. Second, Jesus performs a particular action in an unusually striking and authoritative way, a command-control mode: "I say it. It happens." Third, we are told—by precept or example—to accomplish the same work but in a different way, the classic faith-obedience mode. The mode shifts. There are good biblical reasons to believe that ekballistic healing from demons has been replaced by the classic mode.

Before we start, it is important to note that mode shifts are not unique to the New Testament. The Old Testament gives a striking example of a mode shift in regard to feeding people. When the Israelites wandered in the desert the Lord miraculously provided for their daily needs—the manna appeared each morning and water flowed from the rock. But the moment the Israelites crossed the Jordan, things changed. They ate the last of the manna when they entered the land of milk and honey, fields and fruit trees, springs of running water. A power encounter with natural evil had reversed the curse of the parched desert for forty years, but then the people became farmers and herdsmen. The immediate power mode always served to accomplish particular divine purposes. In the Sinai desert it tested—and, for a few people, taught—daily dependency, fidelity, gratitude, and hope. The spiritual warfare in Sinai was moral, only occasioned by the parched desert and God's mode of providing their physical needs.

These eleven examples that follow build in a rough order, ending with those closest to EMM (ekballistic mode of ministry). Some examples speak of what might seem for some to be relatively minor parts of life: fishing, the weather, taxes. Other examples seem relatively more weighty: forgiving sins, healing the sick, raising the dead. But a consistent pattern will emerge.

1. PAY TAXES

Jesus and the apostle Peter paid their taxes in an unusual way—at least once. Jesus sent Peter fishing with instructions that the payment for their temple tax would be found in the mouth of the first fish Peter caught (Matthew 17:24–27). In this instance the command-control mode served an explicit teaching purpose. The Lord himself need not pay taxes in his own temple; yet, in order not to give offense, he paid the tax in a way that revealed who he was.

Other Scriptures explicitly command us to pay our taxes, assuming we will use more normal methods (Matthew 22:16–22; Romans 13:1–7). The need to pay taxes abides but the mode of raising the money changes. Of course, we are never forbidden to use windfall money to pay our taxes. But Jesus's command-control mode, which created a windfall, is clearly superseded—as it was preceded—by the classic stewardship mode. Work, and pay what is owed.

Notice that the idea of a mode shift between what Jesus does and what we are to do is not really an argument from silence. Scripture gives us no command not to control nature by a word of power in order to get tax money. But because the rest of Scripture teaches and exemplifies a different mode, such a prohibition would be absurd and redundant.

2. CATCH FISH

On two other occasions Jesus also used the authoritative command mode to direct the apostles' fishing trips (Luke 5:4; John 21:3–6). These were power encounters with situational evil: in both cases, the fishermen had worked all night but caught nothing. Jesus used his power to bless his afflicted people, rolling back the curse of futile labor. In both cases, Jesus's command resulted in a staggering catch. The recognition that only the Lord had such power brought varied reactions. Peter was humbled in the first case: "Go away from me, Lord; I am a sinful man." In the second case he jumped into the water in joyful recognition.

In both cases Jesus's mode had a pointed purpose. With fishing, as with paying taxes, Jesus commanded his apostles to do something that revealed his control over the natural world. Are we to follow his mode? Here we have no direct command, only the example of the apostles. When Jesus was not physically present, they fished as they always had. As with the example of the tax money in the fish's mouth—but different from casting out demons and healing—the apostles fished in the power-encounter mode only as the audience and beneficiaries of Jesus's direct command.

3. WALK ON WATER

The Gospels record that Jesus and Peter both walked on the surface of the Sea of Galilee (Matthew 14:24–33). Jesus walked on water because he was the creator of heaven and earth, the maker of water. And Peter walked on water through faith in Jesus as he responded to Christ's command. But Peter began to sink when he lost faith. Jesus rescued and then rebuked him. Jesus used this enacted parable as a living demonstration of the nature of faith. The power encounter also compelled faith directly: "Then those who were in the boat worshiped him, saying, 'Truly you are the Son of God.'"

Today—and throughout the Bible—similar issues of faith are ever present. But now we normally express faith by walking through the deep waters rather than walking on the water. The mode of expressing faith has shifted to the classic mode.

4. FEED THE HUNGRY, GIVE DRINK TO THE THIRSTY

Hunger and thirst—and their many causes—are abiding situational evils. Drought, thorns, locusts, social injustice, enemy invasion, and laziness all can lead to deprivation and even death. The Lord God as a judge made himself known by bringing these evils on those who turned away from him. The Lord God as a savior made himself known by providing for those who took refuge in him. Sometimes he used power encounters: the manna, the quail, Elijah's ravens, the poor widow's bowl of flour and jar of oil. Sometimes he used more "normal" demonstrations of sovereign power: the land flowing with milk and honey, Joseph's prominence in Egypt, the timing of drought and rainfall.

On two occasions Jesus's mode of redressing this evil was to pray and then multiply small amounts of food in order to feed vast crowds. And once he turned water into wine to bless a celebration. Jesus used this mode to accomplish three things: Reveal himself as the Lord, do people tangible good, and invite faith. The miraculous wine at Cana, for example, invited witnesses to ponder Psalm 104:15: The Lord God brings forth "wine that gladdens the heart of man." Jesus displayed his divine power dramatically.

John 6 offers the lengthiest discussion of the purposes of the power-encounter mode. Giving money to the poor could also feed hungry people, a mode that Jesus evidently used routinely (John 13:29). But feeding the hungry on command was an act of love in itself, temporarily sustaining life. And the miracle also provided an opportunity to teach about more profound human needs. The bread that sustained temporal life for a day pointed to the true bread that would sustain life eternally.

What Jesus did in feeding the five thousand typifies other instances. The command-control mode attracted a great deal of attention, revealing that Jesus was at least a prophet of the Lord—another Moses, Elijah, or Elisha—and was perhaps the

Lord himself. As God had given manna to the Israelites in the desert, so now the people ate extraordinary bread. But the mode was not an end in itself, meant to be perpetuated. The mode of Jesus's assaults on situational evil always had the triple focus of being genuine acts of love to needy people, revealing that he was God and Christ incarnate, and prompting faith that people might believe.

We also must feed hungry people, and our mode follows Jesus's example up to a point: we, too, pray. But the Bible teaches a fundamental discontinuity of mode between what Jesus did next and what we do. When we pray the Lord's Prayer, "give us this day our daily bread," we ask God to provide. We either eat the fruit that our own work provides or we eat what others share with us in love. Where Jesus multiplied loaves and fishes, we give to the church, support relief organizations, organize a food cupboard, nurse infants, make supper for our children, show hospitality.

Why do we not use supernatural means to feed the hungry today? Is it simply that we know that by ourselves we cannot? We have no command not to multiply loaves and fishes, but Scripture elsewhere tells us to do something different by both command and example. Paul, for instance, worked diligently to meet his own needs and help the needy (Acts 20:34ff). Ephesians 4:28 tells us to work with our hands so that we can share with those in need. Paul wrote at length to the Corinthians to raise money to help a church in a famine region. The pastoral mode replaced the power-encounter mode.

5. SPEAK WITH GOD'S AUTHORITY

How do humans express God's authority? Jesus spoke with direct, personal authority, saying, "I say to you." He did not speak "as the scribes or the Pharisees" or as we speak. Although we have authority—God's authority—we do not speak in the same way Jesus did. Our authority fundamentally says, "The Bible says . . ." "The Lord says . . ." "God says . . ." This is not weak or impersonal; a sense of gravity and urgency can fill our words: "In the name of the Lord, I solemnly charge you, I plead with you . . ." The Lord's authority can even be unstated rather than overt: "You are killing yourself by what you believe and how you live. Repent or you will die."[2] In any case, ours is a derivative authority, not our own. Or authority is a signpost pointing to the one with all authority in heaven and on earth. Jesus spoke with first-person authority, but we dare not talk that way or else we sin.

6. CALL PEOPLE TO MINISTRY

How did Jesus call people to ministry? He spotted a disciple-to-be and said, "Leave your tax table, leave your nets, come with me." Jesus spoke; the apostles obeyed. Later, Jesus's power encounter with Saul blinded him and knocked him to the ground: "Now get up and go into the city, and you will be told what you must do" (Acts 9:6). Jesus used the command-control mode with unopposable authority.

We, too, must call people and hear the call to ministry. We do not use the command-control mode, but look to Scripture's guidelines in such passages as 1 Timothy 3. Scripture gives objective criteria: character, willingness, experience, reputation, and gifts. We test people, watching their lives over time; we pray to our Lord for wisdom.

---

2. This statement would be on personal authority if we meant, "Repent to me, or I will kill you."

In many of these eleven examples, Jesus used both modes, which is appropriate for the God-man. He first called his disciples in a dramatic and striking way; he then prayed all night before finally selecting twelve to be apostles. Similarly, he ate food that was grown and prepared normally. He crossed the lake in a boat. He quoted Scripture. He used money that had been acquired and donated in normal ways. Even in Jesus's life the command-control mode had a distinct purpose and limited place. The Bible is silent in the sense that it never says *not* to use authoritative commands to call leaders; it is a loud silence, however, because we are given so many instructions about how to use the classic mode.

7. FORGIVE SINS

There are striking continuities and discontinuities between Jesus and us when it comes to dealing with sins. The continuity is at the point of need: there are always people to be forgiven. But Jesus deals with the sins of others quite differently than we do. He provides a substitutionary atonement; he actually and objectively forgives them by acting as the perfect sacrifice on their behalf. He can say, "Father, forgive them" with authority because he speaks as the one who earned the right to forgive people by shedding his own blood for them.

Interestingly, the Gospel of John mentions only one case of ekballistic ministry: "Now the ruler of this world shall be cast out. And I, if I be lifted up from the earth, will draw all men to Myself" (John 12:31–32 NASB). The ultimate exorcism takes place on the cross, where Satan's power to hold us in bondage to sin and death was destroyed. John's lone case of "EMM" delivers the mortal wound to the power and penalty of moral evil.

The discontinuity between Jesus's mode and ours is that we do not die for sin—our own or other people's; we do not create the objective conditions of forgiveness. But the point of continuity is that as recipients of deliverance from the kingdom of darkness, we forgive people as God has forgiven us. We forgive others as *recipients* of Jesus's mode of forgiving: "Forgive each other, just as God in Christ also has forgiven you" (Ephesians 4:32 NASB). Our mode is different not only in the ground of forgiveness, but the process. We can forgive another's sins against us, but we do not forgive the same way God forgives. If a person asks for our forgiveness and is a hypocrite, we still forgive subjectively, holding no grudge against him or her. But the hypocrite will remain unforgiven objectively, because God reads the heart. Jesus does authoritative, objective forgiving; we do personal, subjective forgiving.

8. CONFRONT AND CURSE SIN

The other side of dealing with sin also exemplifies the mode shift. Jesus Christ and the apostles brought wrath to bear immediately. For example, Jesus said to the fig tree, "May you never bear fruit again!" The tree—a picture of unfruitful Israel—withered and died instantly. Peter named the sins of Ananias and Sapphira, who immediately dropped dead. This power encounter deals with moral evil by bringing forward situational evil as an immediate consequence. Imagine that kind of authority operating in a church stewardship campaign today. The pastor could see into the hearts of people. To anyone who fudged a little in order to look good he would simply say, "You're lying and deceiving the Holy Spirit" and would then call the undertaker. But obviously this does not happen because the church is not called to express the just wrath of God in the same way Jesus did.

The need to bring judgment abides. But the Lord and his prophets and apostles command us to exert authority through "normal" means: preaching the Word of God, carrying out church discipline, defending the rights of the oppressed, confronting and warning evildoers. Jesus speaks directly and on his own authority, our authority is derivative and qualified. When Jesus declared divine curses in Matthew 23, he offered no grace; we need to offer grace, the opportunity for repentance and forgiveness.[3]

9. RAISE THE DEAD

Raising the dead is the supreme attack on situational evil, for death is the ultimate logic of all other evils. Jesus raised the dead through both the extraordinary, command-control mode and the normal, dependent-faith mode. In his warfare of compassion against the ultimate situational evil, he commanded, "Young man, I say to you, get up!" and "My child, get up!" and "Lazarus, come out!" (Luke 7:14; Luke 8:54; John 11:43 NIV). But in facing his own moral call to an obedience unto death, he believed, "The Son of Man must . . . be raised up on the third day" (Luke 9:22 NASB) and entrusted himself to him who judges righteously.

How do we raise the dead? We use the second mode, saying, "Believe in the Lord Jesus Christ, who is the resurrection and the life. If you believe in him, you will live even if you die. And if you live and believe in him you shall never die." Similarly we entrust our souls to a faithful creator, Jesus raised the young man of Nain, Jairus's daughter, and Lazarus, but we presume

---

3. In some circumstances—with his disciples or the crowds—Jesus models our way of confronting sin. In others—to the barren fig tree—he acts in the power mode of ultimate judgment.

they later died. But Jesus himself was raised as the firstfruits of the better resurrection of all who love him.

Jesus's three power encounters with death provided tokens of love and signs of divine power that were stunning but temporary. But his central mode of raising the dead through dependent faith in a word of truth works better and lasts longer. Jesus's rarer mode is breathtaking, but it is not finally as powerful as the "normal" mode by which he operates in his universe. This is partly why Jesus says, "Truly, truly, I say to you, whoever believes in me will also do the works that I do; and greater works than these will he do, because I am going to the Father" (John 14:12). Not surprisingly, Jesus then speaks in great detail about prayer, love, and the Holy Spirit. We have received ways of living through the Spirit's power that are more powerful, if sometimes less dramatic, than the command-control mode. When Jesus was on earth, God's glory depended on his immediate authoritative presence. But we are given a mode that can reach throughout the world. We are to raise all who believe in Christ through the preaching of his gospel.

10. CONTROL THE WEATHER

Our final two examples—controlling the weather and healing sickness—are the most pointed because the Bible closely links them to ekballistic ministry. As modern people we may not care about the weather except as an inconvenience; we rarely depend on it directly. But we ought to care, because it affects human life, and God says repeatedly that he controls it.[4] When I spent time in Uganda a number of years ago it seemed so strange to me— a suburban American—when our pastor prayed fervently for

---

4. See Psalms 29, 104, 147.

the rains to come. He had the right idea; I had to grow up to know the God of power.

Jesus, as the Lord God, performed a power encounter with situational evil in dealing with the weather. The specific incident occurred after a notably long day of teaching. Jesus was sleeping in the boat when a fierce storm struck. The boat was foundering before the fearful disciples who woke him. Jesus spoke to the wind and waves, "Quiet! Be still!" His command stilled the storm immediately (Mark 4:35–41, see also Matthew 8:23–27).

We learn our mode of dealing with weather through the many passages that portray God in control of meteorological events and exhibit God's people praying to him. For example, even "Give us this day our daily bread" entails prayers to God regarding the weather. Hardships, whether deserved or undeserved, prompt intercession. The prophet Elijah offers a fascinating example of someone who operated in both the command-control mode and the dependent prayer mode. As an agent of God's judgment, he proclaims, "There will be neither dew nor rain in the next few years except at my word" (1 Kings 17:1 NIV). And yet finally the rain, like the fire, fell in answer to his prayers (1 Kings 18:42; see also 18:36–37). Interestingly, in commanding us how to help sufferers, James 5:17–18 draws an analogy between the weather and sickness, commending to us only Elijah's prayer life for our emulation.

Jesus in the swamping boat operated in the command mode, we operate in the mode of dependent request, asking our Father to work in power. One is not more effective than the other. They are different, but have equally strong effects. For instance, Elijah prayed and there was no rain for three years. He prayed again and the storm came that day. The Ugandan pastor prayed, the seasonal rains arrived several days later. This is God's world.

A comparison of Mark 4:35–41 with Mark 1:23–28 demonstrates how Jesus's power of the weather explicitly connects with his power over demons. Mark 1:23–27 (NIV) describes Jesus's first power encounter: "Just then a man in their synagogue who was possessed by an impure spirit cried out, 'What do you want with us, Jesus of Nazareth? Have you come to destroy us? I know who you are—the Holy One of God!' 'Be quiet!' said Jesus sternly. 'Come out of him!' The impure spirit shook the man violently and came out of him with a shriek. The people were all so amazed that they asked each other, 'What is this? A new teaching—and with authority! He even gives orders to impure spirits and they obey him.'"

Compare this passage to Mark 4:38–41 (NIV), when Jesus calmed the storm. "Jesus was in the stern, sleeping on a cushion. The disciples woke him and said to him, 'Teacher, don't you care if we drown?' He got up, rebuked the wind and said to the waves, 'Quiet! Be still!' Then the wind died down and it was completely calm. He said to his disciples, 'Why are you so afraid? Do you still have no faith?' They were terrified and asked each other, 'Who is this? Even the wind and the waves obey him!'"

The passages are virtually identical thematically and verbally—only the details differ. We can draw at least seven direct parallels. First, both situational evils stormed noisily at Jesus in ways appropriate to a spirit and a gale. Second, Jesus spoke direct rebukes and commands to them. Third, Jesus commanded the same thing in both cases: "Be quiet!" Fourth, both the demon and the storm instantly obeyed: the demon left the man; the wind died down. Fifth, witnesses were stunned, amazed, and afraid, which is the typical response to Jesus's use of the command-control mode. Sixth, in the people's amazement they wondered, "What is this authority? Who is this man?" And seventh, the witnesses commented on what they saw: situational evils—unclean spirits, wind and sea—doing exactly what Jesus told them to do.

The disciples marveled, "Who is this man?" because they knew the Scriptures. Psalm 107:29 (NIV) says, "[The LORD] stilled the storm to a whisper; the waves of the sea were hushed." And the crowds marveled at Jesus' authority over evil spirits because they knew the Scriptures. As we saw throughout the Old Testament, the LORD's permission and will control the evil spirits.

Thus, the command-control mode deals identically with the weather and unclean spirits, two forms of situational evil. They are in the same category: harmful, destructive expressions of the curse.[5] Jesus's mode brought the first taste and glimpse of deliverance from all forms of suffering. The final power encounter with situational evil will come when Jesus returns in glory.

As with the other examples, we see a mode shift for dealing with weather. Jesus speaks, the weather obeys. But we pray to God for deliverance from the sufferings produced by bad weather.

11. HEAL THE SICK

Our final example is the most significant for evaluating EMM. Healing the sick and casting out demons are repeatedly placed in the same category to the extent that Scripture frequently says

---

5. Does this mean that demons are not malicious agents of temptations or false teaching intended to plunge people into bondage to sin? Of course not. The Bible speaks of those who "follow deceiving spirits and things taught by demons" (1 Timothy 4:1 NIV). But in this context, Paul places his emphasis on the *content*—of the teaching and the false teachers. One resists such demonically inspired lies by resisting the message and messenger and holding fast to truth. As we have seen repeatedly, EMM is uncalled for with moral evil.

that Jesus heals people of demons.[6] Sickness is a great evil, a foretaste of death. Jesus heals the sick by speaking word. Then the blind see, the deaf hear, the lame walk, the fevered cool off, the withered regain strength.

Jesus was moved by compassion to alleviate physical suffering. He brought both relief and joy to the afflicted. These good works are repeatedly spoken of as signs of Jesus's identity, the one who "heals all your diseases, who redeems your life from the pit," who "bind[s] up the brokenhearted [and] comfort[s] all who mourn" (Psalm 103:3–4; Isaiah 61:1–2).

Healings—both before and after they occurred—were repeatedly linked to Jesus's call to place faith in him as healer. On several occasions Jesus also explicitly used healing power to establish his authority to forgive sins. As often is the case, the Gospel of John throws the most extensive light on the wider purposes of Jesus's mode. In John 9 Jesus healed the blind man to reveal the works of God, invite faith, and drive unbelief into the open. In John 11 Jesus raised Lazarus to teach a bigger lesson: "I am the resurrection and the life." The command-control mode compelled faith; it also hardened unbelief into murderous intent.

Should we also use the command-control mode to heal? Scripture explicitly instructs us otherwise. The normal mode of healing in both the Old and New Testaments is to pray, placing primary reliance on God, and then to employ medical means. Prayerful faith in God the healer lays the foundation. Perhaps the best illustration of the classic mode of healing occurs in Isaiah 38. King Hezekiah is near death from an infection, and prays with great anguish of heart to God for deliverance from his affliction. God hears him. Medical treatment—applying a

---

6. See, for example, the summary statement in Matthew 4:23–24 and a specific incident in Matthew 12:22.

poultice to the boil—follows (Isaiah 38:21), but putting God first is crucial. Another king's suffering warns against forgetting to put first things first. Asa became severely diseased in his feet, but "even in his illness he did not seek help from the LORD, but only from the physicians. Then . . . Asa died and rested with his ancestors" (2 Chronicles 16:12–13 NIV).

Some will respond that it is an argument from silence to say that we do not heal using Jesus's command-control mode. After all, they point out, there is no command not to heal using Jesus's mode just as there is no negative command for any of the previous ten examples. But Scripture specifically tells us to approach sickness a different way. James 5:14–16 teaches the church what methodology to use. "Is any one of you sick? He should call the elders of the church to pray over him and anoint him with oil in the name of the Lord. And the prayer offered in faith will make the sick person well; the Lord will raise him up. If he has sinned, he will be forgiven. Therefore confess your sins to each other and pray for each other so that you may be healed. The prayer of a righteous man is powerful and effective."

Four points stand out in this passage about how we should ask God to work powerfully on behalf of sick people. First, the shepherds of the church should get involved in a personal way. General prayers from the pulpit are not sufficient; prayer for the sick is hands-on, face-to-face work.

Second, sickness often creates a counseling context, so confession of sins is mentioned. Situational evils, sickness included, frequently bring varied sins to the surface. Sickness may be a judgment on sin, either as a natural consequence or a specific punishment. Or it may occasion temptations to sin: fears, despair, self-pity, selfishness, anger, escapism, regret, grumbling, trusting medicine, trusting faith healers, denying reality, and so forth. Or sickness may prompt self-examination that brings awareness of previously unseen sins. Sickness creates tremendous counseling opportunities to minister the grace of Christ and to help people grow in faith and obedience.

Third, Scripture never despises the use of medical means. James 5 may directly encourage the use of medical means when it speaks of "anointing him with oil in the name of the Lord." In English this sounds like a ceremonial anointing. But the word James uses for "anoint" is not the word typically used for spiritual or ceremonial anointing. The word used usually describes rubbing in ointments medicinally or using oils to cleanse and groom the human body. Oils were the basis of the most common medical treatments. If this is James's intent, then his exhortation is to employ medical means as an act of faith in God. "In the name of the Lord" stresses that medical treatment must not be received as an act of faith in medicine but as an act of faith in the Lord who heals.

Fourth, James 5 encourages robust prayer by giving the example of Elijah. The prayer mode calls on the same power—God's—that the command-control mode also expressed. Jesus did healings one way; the Bible tells us to do them another way.

A MODE SWITCH FOR DEMONIC AFFLICTIONS?

Matthew, Mark, Luke, and Acts portray Jesus and the apostles using the command-control mode to address sickness, the weather, paying taxes, speaking with personal authority, and so forth. The rest of the New Testament, following the main approach in the Old Testament, exemplifies and commands a different mode. Is there a similar mode switch for dealing with demons associated with ailments and afflictions?

We certainly will not be surprised to find a mode shift. Scripture is "silent" on the issue in the same way it is silent on paying taxes, performing resurrections, or stilling storms by words of command. The silence thunders. The mode of addressing demonically induced sufferings reverts to the classic mode: live the Christian life of receptive faith and active obedience in the midst of life's hardships.

EMM, similar to every other example, served temporary purposes. Scripture gives no command to perpetuate EMM. Similarly, the epistles consistently evidence the classic-mode approach to demonic (and other) sufferings, analogous to the Old Testament. But it is worth noting that Scripture does not abound with examples of demonic suffering, outside of the examples from the Old Testament and the Gospels already discussed. Most of the Bible's attention is directed to the true spiritual warfare with the powers of sin, something that never involved EMM in the Gospels or anywhere else.

The modern demon-deliverance ministries are predicated on two fundamental errors. First, they misread the biblical record and fail to distinguish between moral evil and situational evil. They cast out "demons" of moral evil, something neither taught nor illustrated anywhere in Scripture. Second, they fail to reckon with the general mode shift away from the command-control mode and toward the classic mode.

There are serious theological and pastoral consequences of going beyond Scripture. If we are to address one situational evil—spirits that cause affliction—differently from how we address every other situational evil, we will need good reasons and clear instructions. And if we are to widen the use of the EMM mode dramatically—supposing that spirits infiltrate the human personality, take up residence, and secretly exacerbate and constrain patterns of sin and unbelief—we will need utterly compelling reasons.

EMM advocates are not following Jesus's model when they link demonization with sin patterns. Jesus never does this. In effect, they advocate their own radical mode switch—a new use for EMM as a necessary supplement to Jesus's classic mode—with neither direct biblical warrant nor the any analogy from Scripture. Neither the Old Testament nor Jesus nor the letters in the New Testament say that EMM addresses the moral dilemma of our hearts, our bondage to sin, or our warfare with Satan as a would-be lord. The way of progressive sanctification in the face of life's troubles is a different way.

Christian Counseling & Educational Foundation

CCEF's mission is to restore Christ to

counseling and counseling to the church

by thinking biblically about the issues

of living in order to equip the church to

meet counseling-related needs.

For other resources like these,
please visit **ccef.org**